VIVID AND CONTINUOUS

VIVID &

CONTINUOUS

Essays and Exercises
for Writing Fiction

JOHN M^cNALLY

UNIVERSITY OF IOWA PRESS, IOWA CITY

University of Iowa Press, Iowa City 52242
Copyright © 2013 by John McNally
www.uiowapress.org
Printed in the United States of America
Design by April Leidig

The University of Iowa Press is a member of Green Press Initiative
and is committed to preserving natural resources.

Printed on acid-free paper

Library of Congress Cataloging-in-Publication Data
McNally, John, 1965–
Vivid and continuous: essays and exercises
for writing fiction / John McNally.
p. cm.
Includes index.
ISBN 978-1-60938-156-1, 1-60938-156-4 (pbk)
ISBN 978-1-60938-157-8, 1-60938-157-2 (e-book)
1. Fiction—Authorship. 2. Authorship—Handbooks,
manuals, etc. 3. Creative writing—Handbooks,
manuals, etc. I. Title.
PN3355.M377 2013
808.3—dc23 2012028420

for Holly Carver

We recreate, with minor and for the most part unimportant changes, the vivid and continuous dream the writer worked out in his mind (revising and revising until he got it right) and captured in language so that other human beings, whenever they feel like it, may open his book and dream that dream again.
—**John Gardner,** *On Becoming a Novelist*

CONTENTS

Acknowledgments xi

Introduction xiii

Writing 1

The Ideal Reader 8

Subject Matter 14

Beginnings 31

Titles 40

The Narrator's Likeability 46

Minor Characters 53

Immediacy 63

Pop Culture 99

Humor 102

Neighborhoods 112

The Imitative Fallacy 118

Subtext 127

Gestation 132

Humility 141

Further Reading 149

Index 159

ACKNOWLEDGMENTS

EARLIER VERSIONS of the following chapters first appeared in the these publications: "Humor" appeared as "Humor Incarnate" in *Winding Roads: Exercises in Writing Creative Nonfiction* (Longman, 2008), edited by Diane Thiel; "Beginnings" appeared as "McNally on Story Beginnings" in *Behind the Short Story: From First Draft to Final Draft* (Longman, 2006), edited by Todd James Pierce and Ryan G. Van Cleave; "Minor Characters" appeared as "The Boy that Had Created the Disturbance: Reflections on Minor Characters in Life and *The Catcher in the Rye*" in *With Love and Squalor: 14 Writers Respond to the Work of J. D. Salinger* (Broadway Books, 2001), edited by Kip Kotzen and Thomas Beller; and "Subtext" appeared as "The Secret Life of Subtext" in *Passages North* (2007). My gratitude to the editors of these textbooks, anthologies, and journals.

Some of these essays grew out of talks I've given at AWP conferences. My thanks to fellow panelists and audience members for the opportunity to discuss and refine my ideas.

Most of these essays began as extemporaneous lectures I've given in my fiction writing classes with one notable exception. The germ for "Beginnings" can be traced to the fall of 1987 when I took a course with Frank Conroy, who often spoke of the first page of a story as a contract made with the reader. My own ramblings on the subject are the result of having thought quite a bit about Frank's words in the intervening twenty-five years.

If not for my students, I would never have had the chance to articulate any of the ideas in this book. Every semester brings a new crop of writers, many of whom have never written a word of fiction, and it's a fresh challenge each time to encourage students to think more deeply about the words they're putting on the page. I've certainly learned a lot from teaching all these years, and I have only my students to thank for the hundreds of times I've stood in front of them to try out these ideas when they were embryonic.

Three writers were kind enough to answer my questions on process: Elizabeth Stuckey-French, Jonathan Evison, and Alan Heathcock.

Thank you to Melissa Cox for her bibliographic work.

I have had the pleasure of working with Holly Carver on four books now. She has been an exceedingly patient editor, always encouraging. I'm a lucky writer to have worked with someone so smart and generous.

During the last few days of piecing together this book, trying to fill in missing pieces, I posted a couple of questions on Facebook, asking for very specific recommendations for short stories and novels, and my friends responded quickly and smartly, oftentimes with titles I should have remembered but didn't. How could I have forgotten *that* story? In the end, I could use only five or six suggestions, even though they were all excellent. What can I say? I have friends with good taste. At the end of the thread for my last question, the writer Cathy Day sent me a link to what she calls "toolbox stories," stories that she carries around in her head. It was funny to see how many of *her* toolbox stories were also *my* toolbox stories. But there were other stories that I either hadn't read in many years or had never read, and so her list prompted me to start pulling those stories off my shelves or tracking them down. I encourage all of you to put together your own toolbox stories, those stories that you return to time and again, the ones that have taught you how to be a writer. And then pass that list along to others—many others. After all, it's how we keep what we do alive.

Here's where you can find Cathy Day's toolbox stories: http://cathyday .com/teaching/toolbox-stories/

INTRODUCTION

EVERY SEMESTER in my beginning fiction writing class, after a discussion of craft, a student will ask, "Do you *really* think about all these things before you sit down to write?"

Their fear is that attention to craft will take the fun out of writing. I explain to them that it's like playing pool: you work on a bank shot, you watch other players far better than you, and you spend countless hours thinking about the shot. And then one night—after endless hours of practice, observation, and rumination—you run the table. You've *internalized* what you need to do, and you simply do it without thinking. Writers, not unlike pool players, spend years working on their game: writing stories, reading as writers, studying under published writers, considering the cause and effect of craft. The more they do this, the more likely that their control of craft will become second nature. My hope is that this book will help bring the aspiring writer, if only ever-so-slightly, closer to reaching that goal.

My first rule: Don't be overwhelmed by all of this!

When I took my first creative writing course as a sophomore at Southern Illinois University, I had no idea what I was doing. I continued taking creative writing courses, and if I was a little less clueless each semester, it was mostly because of my professors, all of whom were accomplished writers who gently pointed out my clichés or the fact that I didn't understand the first thing about point of view, but it was also because of a book I had found in the university bookstore, John Gardner's posthumously published *The Art of Fiction*.

I eventually became fascinated by John Gardner because he had taught at Southern Illinois, because he had spent so many years writing unpublished novels before landing his first book contract and subsequently hitting it big as a best-selling novelist, and because he had died in a tragic, somewhat mysterious motorcycle accident. Later still, when I returned to Southern Illinois to teach fiction writing, I tracked down Gardner's old house on Boskydell Road with its dragon sculpture on its front lawn, and wondered which books he had written there. By then, I had met numerous people in town who had met or known Gardner, including my then-girlfriend, whose stepfather had been friends with him, and I was eager to hear anything anyone had to offer up on the man.

But I'm getting ahead of myself, because when I first discovered *The Art of Fiction* as a sophomore, I didn't know who John Gardner was, and the first time I read his book, I resisted most of what he had to say. His personality oozed from every sentence, and I found him to be snotty, opinionated, and elitist. His theories on writing were presented as definite, and he was often brutal in his assessments of beginning writers who failed to live up to his standards. Here's a typical passage from the book:

> Strictly speaking, frigidity characterizes the writer who presents serious material, then fails to carry through—fails to treat it with the attention and seriousness it deserves. I would extend the term to mean a further cold-heartedness as well, the given writer's inability to recognize the seriousness of things in the first place, the writer who turns away from real feeling, or sees only the superficialities in a conflict of wills, or knows no more about love, beauty, or sorrow than one might learn from a Hallmark card.

Ouch! (Gardner, it should be noted, was no slouch when it came to doling out harsh assessments, even to his own detriment, as when he strongly criticized many of his contemporaries in his fascinating book *On Moral Fiction*.)

For whatever reason—call it masochism—I kept returning to *The Art of Fiction*, intrigued by it, and then a funny thing happened. The more I wrote, the more I warmed to it. And once I began teaching, I saw with perfect clarity why he wrote the things he did, because I began to see in abundance all of the problems Gardner cited. Over time I became a full-fledged Gardner convert, if not downright evangelical in my enthusiasm, handing out copies of the book to those I had hoped to convert, reading long passages aloud in class, and invoking Gardner's name with reverence. One of my older copies of *The Art of Fiction* (I own probably a dozen) has been highlighted in four different colors; it appears to have been soaked in a tub and then run over by a Mack truck. This is the copy I read from to my students, and like the raging preacher on a street corner, I will sometimes hold the book up as I recite from memory.

THE TITLE OF THIS BOOK, *Vivid and Continuous*, is a nod to Mr. Gardner, not only for the aesthetic theory espoused in the epigraph that opens this book but also as an acknowledgment of the shadow Gardner casts over my own ideas. It wouldn't take much effort to trace back most of my precepts to *The Art of Fiction* or to Gardner's other essential book on writing, *On Becoming a Novelist*. But I also owe a debt to Gardner for teaching me that it's okay to be blunt as long as it's honest and in the service of trying to help. Gardner may have been opinionated, but those opinions were well-earned from his years as a writer and a teacher, and he was unafraid to take a stance and stick with it. In the end, those two books on writing were ultimately encouraging, and over the years I have met innumerable writers, especially of my generation, who cite them as the most influential books on writing they've read. Twenty-seven years after I bought my first copy in the university bookstore, I still keep a copy of *The Art of Fiction* near me when I write. It's the closest I've found to a holy book for writers.

In *Vivid and Continuous*, I adhere to the doctors' Hippocratic oath, *primum non nocere*: first, do no harm. Reading this book will not injure you in any permanent way, nor should it crush your spirit. I set out to write a book on the craft of fiction writing that didn't hide my personality, a book where I could weave my own experiences as a writer and teacher through the more technical discussions of craft and where I could give myself permission to be blunt. As for the subjects that I cover in this book, I tried not to duplicate the many fine books on fiction writing already on the market, books that cover the essentials, like point of view, characterization, setting, and dramatization, although I readily admit to having been influenced by fiction writing textbooks that were a seminal part of my own education. Mostly, I have tried to explore here subjects found as footnotes in those books but subjects nonetheless that I find myself spending considerable time discussing in the classroom. Therefore, I wrote this slim volume with the idea that it might be a supplement to a beginning fiction writing class or, possibly, as the sole text for an upper-level or graduate-level course. The novels and short stories cited within each chapter are not meant to represent the wide range of writers tackling these issues; they are merely the examples to which I have returned time and again for illumination, or the ones that, over the years, have best illustrated the lessons I want to make for my students. At the end of this book, you'll find three lists for further reading: the writer's life, the writer's craft, and a few of my own favorite novels and short story collections.

I have also included exercises at the end of each chapter. Mostly, these exercises are designed to reinforce the chapter's point, but they may also serve as a catalyst for a new story. Some of the best stories that my students write grow out of exercises. A few of these exercises are designed to purge you of ineffective technique by gorging on it. Want to lose your appetite for hamburgers? Eat a dozen in a single sitting. You probably won't want to look at another hamburger for several years.

In some of these essays, I take a more personal approach than in others. For instance, I occasionally cite my own books and stories, not because I view them as the height of artistic achievement (they're not), but because I know best what was going through my mind as I wrote them. I also write about my life because I don't see a way to separate the personal from the artistic. For me, the two are intrinsically intertwined. I suppose I could have written a more detached textbook, but that's not what I wanted to do here.

I've spent almost three decades thinking about all of the things I've stuffed into these pages. Like a baton passed from one runner to another, the germs of my own theories on writing were first handed to me by my professors, or they came from published interviews with writers, or I discovered them in books on writing, most notably John Gardner's. And so I pass the baton on to you now with the hope that this book, whether you agree with any of it or not, prompts you to think more deeply about a variety of issues in your own work, all the while pushing you toward writing more meaningful, accomplished short stories and novels.

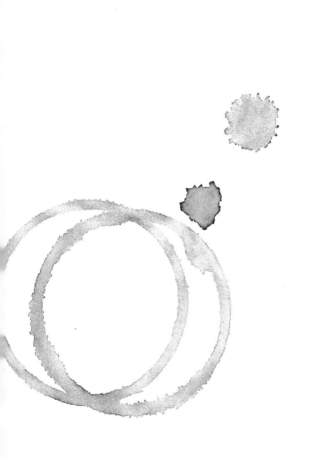

VIVID AND CONTINUOUS

Writing

WHAT'S YOUR PROCESS LIKE? When do you write? Do you have a routine? Do you write in the morning or at night? Do you write every day? Do you write longhand or type? How much do you write each day? How many hours a day do you write? Do you stand or sit when you write? Do you gauge a day's work by words, pages, or time spent writing? Do you write seven days a week? Do you have a specific place where you write, or can you write anywhere? Do you write with the door open or shut? Do you play music while you write? Do you shower before you write? Do you write in your underwear?

During nearly every post-reading Q&A, someone will ask the writer one of these questions, but what they're really asking is, "What's your secret?" The secret is that there is no secret. Most writers do, in fact, develop idiosyncratic habits, but they do so because it works for them. And by "works," I mostly mean that it keeps them going; it gets them from one day to the next. I do believe that some writers' processes have effects on their writing, but by and large the reason we do the things we do is because it makes the experience endurable if not actually pleasant, the way a child might need a particular blanket to sleep with at night. It's not that the child *couldn't* sleep without it, but it makes falling asleep easier. The great thing about being a writer is that we don't have to give up our blanket.

Time Is on Your Side

My own habits have changed over the years, most notably in regard to the one thing that probably does actually affect the writing itself: the time of day I choose to write. I used to be a night person, writing from midnight until five in the morning, but that was back when I was a student and could sleep all day long without consequences. Once I started working for a living, I couldn't possibly maintain that schedule, so I eventually, slowly made the transition to writing in the mornings. In both instances, I wrote when I was groggy, barely awake, because I believe that my best work comes from the unconscious mind, and that the best way to tap into the unconscious mind is to write when the thought process is still nearest to the dream-state. I want my prose to be lucid, but I want to surprise myself by letting the unconscious mind inform the work. Once I'm fully awake, I start thinking about what I have to do that day, e-mails I need to answer, bills I need to pay, tasks I need to take care of—and once all of those things begin to intrude, my brain blocks out the element of surprise and the writing becomes calculated, about as far away from the dream-state as it can get. Gone are the surprising connections. Gone are the enigmatic details. I might as well try hammering a nail through a wall of steel.

The time of day a writer writes is not insignificant. Cynthia Ozick wrote at night. In an interview published in the *Paris Review*, Ozick says, "Most social life begins in the evening when I'm just starting. So when I go out at night, it means I lose a whole day's work." Jonathan Evison, author of *West of Here*, says, "I like early morning, five A.M.-ish, because I have no distractions at that hour, and if I force myself to get up that early, you can bet I'm not going to procrastinate." Alan Heathcock, author of *Volt*, says, "I write from the time I get my three kids off to school, to the time they come home. I write Monday through Friday. Having grown up in a working-class town in the Southland area of south Chicago, I'm always intensely aware that buddies of mine are police officers or pipe fitters or office stiffs, going to do their work, day after day, and that they would have nothing but disdain for me if I treated my writing like anything but a job (even though it's much more than a job)."

Rarely will you hear a writer say, "It doesn't make a difference what time of day I write." Routine, routine, routine: a writer finds a routine that works and, barring life's interferences, sticks with it.

Bean Counting

I try to write at least two typed pages a day. If I'm really deep into a novel or have built up enough steam, I'll write more—four or five pages, as many as fifteen, although I believe that the laws of diminishing returns kick in early, and the more I write, the worse it gets. If I can write at least two typed pages a day for three hundred days a year, that brings my yearly total to six hundred pages, which is the length of two moderately sized books. Of course, most of what I write I have to throw away, and most of the year is spent revising rather than churning out pages, but still . . . a few pages each day will add up over time. I once tried writing an entire novel in a month, and I succeeded, except that my agent couldn't sell it, which said to me that I needed to slow the hell down. The novel was an experiment. The problem was that it *read* like an experiment.

Everyone works at a different pace. "I like to get ten pages a day," writes Stephen King in *On Writing*, "which amounts to 2,000 words. That's 180,000 words over a three-month span, a goodish length for a book—something in which the reader can get happily lost, if the tale is done well and stays fresh." Thomas Wolfe, like King, wrote whale-sized novels. In *The Letters of Thomas Wolfe*, Wolfe claims to a friend that he was he was churning out 3,000 words per day but was hoping to increase to 4,000. As documented in *Working Days: The Journals of The Grapes of Wrath*, John Steinbeck created for himself a complex-sounding equation, explained in his journal entry on June 11, 1938: "The placing of an optional page on Saturday is to try to maintain a certain writing speed. Then if for any reason I miss a day (and I probably shall), there will be days piled up. Two days a month, in fact, to draw on. Two weeks gone now out of twenty. Eighteen weeks to go. I figure about 200,000 words and I have 10,000 words a week as a minimum. Today I will have one spare day in case anything happens. I hope it won't, but if it does."

Most writers I know have more modest goals, like Jonathan Evison, who is happy with one typed page per day. And not every writer believes in word or page count. Elizabeth Stuckey-French, author of *The Revenge of the Radioactive Lady*, writes, "When I'm writing the draft of a novel, I have to make myself write for 2 hours each weekday." According to Alan Heathcock, "I don't believe a page count is appropriate. I set daily goals which have more to do with solving a certain narrative issue, writing a particular scene, extracting insight from a moment. I'm not a quantity guy. I'm a quality guy. And writing is not a race. Writing 5,000 words shabbily can't compete with 200 words written with precision and passion."

What's Your Poison?

I usually start my day, prior to writing, drinking an ice-cold bottle of frappuccino, but I'm trying to quit. The caffeine/sugar rush is great for the first half hour, but it doesn't take long before I crash. Some people light a cigarette before typing their first words of the day; others start filling themselves with vats of coffee. Notice how the unhealthy part of the process precedes the writing. Is writing so daunting, so excruciating that we actually need to brace ourselves with stimulants or depressants first? Or are we playing a role? After all, in nearly every movie about a writer ever made, the writer is portrayed as a hard-drinking, cigarette-smoking troublemaker. Don't believe me? Rent the Humphrey Bogart movie *In a Lonely Place* and then let's talk.

I had read somewhere that William Faulkner would wake up early, start drinking whiskey, and hammer out dozens of pages of a novel, so I decided to give it a go. I was in graduate school, still young enough to think this was a good idea. I dubbed it my "Faulkner Day." I started writing and drinking around nine in the morning, and I wrote several pages on a legal pad, but the next day when I looked over what I had written, I saw that much of it was illegible, despite the increased size of the handwriting, and that what *was* legible wasn't any good. My one and only Faulkner Day was a failure. And the truth is that I can't even write with a hangover, which is why, now that I'm older and (I hope) wiser, I rarely drink, because I hate wasting writing days, those days being the very thing I spend so much time and energy trying to hoard. It's a romantic image, isn't it, pouring a glass of your favorite liquor as you stare gloomily at your blank computer screen, but I suspect the idolization of someone like Charles Bukowski, whose drunken exploits have been dramatized in two movies, has ruined more than one promising young writer's career.

Location, Location, Location

I used to be able to write anywhere. When I was an undergrad at Southern Illinois University and writing my first short stories, I would work for several hours at the library until it closed for the day and then I would wander over to the student union and write at a table near the escalator, until that building closed as well. I used to write on trains, in hospital waiting areas, in dorm rooms. These days, I can't write in public or even in my office on campus, where I'm likely to see people I might prefer to avoid. Instead, I have an office at home where I do almost all my work, but even this setup isn't without problems. I have several dogs and cats, and the dogs, in particular, have become more and more demanding of my time and attention. I love my dogs. I do. But on days when they're acting out, it's difficult to get done what I need to get done—that is, until I bought a used Airstream trailer. When I bought it, it hadn't yet crossed my mind to use it as a makeshift office, but one day, on a whim, I carried my computer and books out there, and that's what it has since become. My daily output has increased by at least ten percent. And there are no distractions, save for a squirrel running over the roof every fifteen minutes. Ironically, during a seven-month period when I'd *had* to live in a camping trailer due to unemployment, I barely wrote ten pages. In that instance, I couldn't escape the smallness of the trailer. Using a trailer as my office, however, is a wholly different experience. I at least have a house to which I can return now.

Is a camping trailer the new writer's garret? Perhaps. Alan Heathcock owns one, too: "My ritual is to walk out my front door and walk around the house to the side drive where my trailer/writing studio is parked. It's a 1967 Roadrunner Travel Trailer, with all the original wood, was once an Idaho State Police surveillance vehicle. I find leaving the house, even for that very short commute, makes me take the writing less like a hobby and more like a job."

And maybe that's it: It isn't so much *where* one writes as it is having a place to write that's separate from where one lives. A room of one's own, as it were.

Weapon of Choice

When I first began writing, I wrote in longhand and then typed up what I'd written, using a cast-iron Royal typewriter from the 1940s, pecking out my words with two fingers. After the manual typewriter—and after taking typing lessons—I bought a Smith Corona typewriter, and then a Brother typewriter, and then a Smith Corona word processor, and then, finally, a long series of computers, all of them utterly forgettable. In the early 1990s, I began typing directly onto the computer. After nearly twenty years of writing this way—from brain to computer—I have begun writing in longhand again. I have even purchased a refurbished IBM Selectric typewriter from the early 1970s. In other words, I'm moving in reverse. Why? The main reason is that (for me, at least) the writing process is different when I use a pen instead of a keyboard. The sentences have different rhythms. The prose takes less time to revise. With a computer, I'm a fast writer; I've hammered out as many as twenty pages of prose in a single sitting. I couldn't write that much in longhand if I tried . . . and that's a good thing! Why write twenty crappy pages when I could have written two or three worthwhile ones?

When asked by the *Paris Review* what implements he wrote with, T. C. Boyle replied, "I use my toenails actually—collect them, hammer them down, mold them into shape, but I guess you want a straight answer."

I was in the audience when Boyle was asked that question, and the audience wanted not only the straight answer but the definitive one, because our deepest hope, as aspiring writers, is that we, too, will write a masterpiece if only we find the right time of day, the right implement with which to write it down, the magical number of words to produce, the perfect place for the muse to visit us, when in fact there is no right anything. There is, when all is said and done, only that which works for you.

EXERCISES

1. Try writing in different locations. For instance, try writing in solitude and then try writing somewhere busy, like a coffee shop. Do you notice any differences? Does one place work better for you?

2. Try writing at different times of the day, particularly early morning (earlier than you would normally wake up) and late night (later than you normally stay awake). Any differences? Any preferences?

3. If you normally write one way, try another way. For instance, if you use a computer for first drafts, try composing your first draft longhand. Or try—take a deep breath—a typewriter. Is one easier? Is one more polished? Is one preferable?

The Ideal Reader

I HAVE NEVER SAT DOWN to write a story or novel and thought, "Okay, so who's my audience going to be?" When asked by others who my audience is, I'll sometimes say, "Writers don't choose their audience; their audience chooses them," which sounds good and which, to a certain point, I believe to be true, but which ultimately is a cop-out of an answer. The truth is that we do, consciously or unconsciously, hone our stories and novels in such a way that we can't help making certain readers more receptive to our work while excluding or distancing other readers.

When you're in a creative writing workshop, especially an MFA program, it's almost impossible *not* to write with your immediate audience in mind. Even if you tell yourself that you're not going to write for that particular audience, the very fact that you're conscious of whom you're *not* writing for is evidence of the role which that particular audience is still having in your work. To be conscious of *not* writing for an audience is, to my mind, an act of writing with that particular audience still in mind.

A creative writing workshop only magnifies and compounds the problem. Even at the undergraduate level, the student often becomes aware that the professor is the target audience since she's the one grading the story. And it's true: how could she *not* be the target audience if she's the one lecturing on craft, correcting mistakes, and assigning stories to read? Not surprisingly, my breakthrough story—the first story of mine that garnered some attention and opened a few doors—was written the summer after I graduated from my MFA program. It was the first time in five years that a workshop audience wasn't looming in my future. I wrote that story as though I was to be its only reader, and it was a liberating experience. Who cared what anyone else thought? The result was that I had written, for the first time, a short story that seemed organic—not constructed, not fabricated. Because it seemed organic, it also seemed more honest. Where the story came from, I couldn't have said. The opening sentences came to me as I was falling asleep, and I wrote the first page of the story in the dark—literally in the dark.

Over the past twenty-plus years now, since graduating from my MFA program, I've thought a lot about audience, and for me, audience boils down to "ideal readers." Who are my ideal readers? I can't say that I've come to any of these conclusions consciously, but I have, at long last, narrowed down my ideal readers to three people.

My First Ideal Reader

This may sound odd, but my first ideal reader is my mother.

My mother passed away in 1988 while I was finishing up my MFA, so she had read only a handful of my very early stories. Nonetheless, on those rare occasions when I think about my ideal reader, my mother is who most often comes to mind. The more I tell you about her, the odder my choice may at first seem. She was an extremely intelligent woman with a very limited education. In fact, she didn't go to school beyond the eighth grade. She had grown up in a sharecropping family in Tennessee and began picking cotton when she was three. My mother was embarrassed by her lack of education and often referred to herself as "not smart," which couldn't have been further from the truth. Her psychological acuity was sharper than most academics I've met, and she had the gift of a natural storyteller, something I wouldn't fully appreciate until long after she had died and I had been teaching creative writing for a number of years. She told wonderful stories about her childhood, and even though I'd heard those stories a dozen times or more, I never tired of hearing her tell them. What she knew was how to be patient. She was never superfluous in detail, and she never took unnecessary detours, but she never rushed the telling, providing just enough details to set the scene while pushing the narrative forward. She understood dramatization by giving the actual dialogue of other people in the scene, and she intuitively understood narrative arc: her stories always had a beginning, middle, and an end. The stories were complex, morally ambiguous. Even when the closure involved a wrong being dealt with, the stories were never preachy or moralistic. There were always shades of gray, and the people she told me about were always complex and often haunting, like her father, a violent man who favored my mother and never hit her as he did his other children.

As an adult, my mother rarely read anything other than romance novels, but I knew she wasn't satisfied with them. On more than one occasion, she would express disappointment in them, saying, "I know what's going to happen in them, so I don't even know why I bother." My mother also suffered from depression, but we weren't the sort of family to talk openly about such things, let alone acknowledge that we were suffering from it, so she never described it as depression. As an adult myself now, I suspect that her unfulfilled intellectual potential—a potential she didn't even realize she had due to her stunted education—contributed to her depression. When I was an undergraduate and reading for the first time the works of great writers, I brought home books I thought she might like. The first was William Faulkner's *As I Lay Dying*. It's not Faulkner's most difficult book, but, like most of Faulkner's work, it's not as accessible as the work of other writers. I didn't tell my mother that Faulkner was a "difficult writer." I gave her the book because there was something about it that reminded me of the stories she had told me about her own upbringing in the South. My mother read the book and enjoyed it. The story *did* resonate with her. We talked for a while about the things in the book that mirrored her own experiences. Never once did she say that it was a difficult book, nor did I get the feeling that Faulkner's prose alienated her from the story. That same year, I also gave her Richard Wright's *Black Boy*, a much more accessible book stylistically, and again she appreciated the story. Wright's story, as with Faulkner's, resonated with her own experiences, and listening to her talk about the book suggested to me that her reading experience had been a more fulfilling one than when she read romance novels. And so I gave her more books to read—among them John Steinbeck's *East of Eden* and Raymond Carver's *Cathedral*—and I eventually showed her some of my own stories.

What my mother reminds me, even now, is that it's possible to write a complex, intelligent book without alienating your reader. And so when I write a novel like *After the Workshop*, which is about the "rarefied world of writing and publishing" (as some editors who rejected the book referred to it), I would have wanted someone like my mother, who knew nothing whatsoever about that world, to be able to pick it up and enjoy it. It's really as simple as that. I don't want to alienate my reader, nor do I have any desire to impress my colleagues. And so my hope is that while the world I'm writing about may be "rarefied"—or whatever word someone wants to call it—the heart of the story is (I hope) universal, and the people in it are (again I hope) recognizable. The biggest compliment I can receive is when someone from my old neighborhood comes up to me at a signing and says, "I haven't read a book since high school, but I couldn't put this one down," or "I don't have much time to read, but my brother gave me this book, and I read it in a day." Whenever this happens, I think, *Yes, I've found my ideal reader!* If my colleagues—all English literature professors—enjoy my books, that's fine, too, but truth be told, they're *not* my ideal readers. I'm sure *some* of them (not all) think I'm not experimental enough or that the ideas in my books aren't as challenging as they could be or that my books aren't nihilistic enough. Well, too bad. If I ever write a book that wouldn't have been accessible to my mother, shame on me.

I'm not saying that every writer should have the same ideal reader that I do. If someone wants to be the next John Barth or Thomas Pynchon or Toni Morrison, that's perfectly fine, but in that instance your ideal reader should probably be your American Lit professor and not your mother, unless they are one and the same. I'm also not saying that my mother would have *liked* everything that I've written. In fact, she had noted in the few stories that she read that my characters swore too much. Point taken. The litmus test for me is about not alienating my reader; it's not necessarily about pleasing her.

My Second Ideal Reader

This ideal reader is really more of a composite than an individual: all of my former writing professors (those teachers I admire, at least). Having this particular (collective) ideal reader has nothing to do with imitating one's teachers and everything to do with maintaining a certain standard. Whenever I write, and particularly when I revise, I hear a cacophony of voices, the voices of my former writing professors, and the things I hear them saying are the things they actually said in the many classes I took with them. Richard Russo, one of my undergraduate writing teachers, guided me through point of view and, when I was turning in stories that were strikingly similar in tone, gently let me know that a reader would tire over the course of a book full of stories that were so alike. Frank Conroy, my first writing teacher in graduate school, painstakingly questioned every choice a writer made. Why do you need a semicolon there? Why is this in the first person? Wouldn't it be better in the third person? Why the paragraph break here? Allan Gurganus brilliantly trimmed away needless words in my stories and pointed out clunky transitions.

There were more teachers than those three, many more, and they all offered good advice. It's been impossible to shake their voices, but I'm grateful that I can't because they were right. Their advice would have been good advice for *any* writer. As for being ideal readers, I'm not writing for them so much as I'm writing to their high standards. If my prose is slack, I often think, *Conroy wouldn't have let me get away with this.* If my story lacks immediacy, I remember Gurganus's pen marks on my stories, all those arrows and crossed-out passages and wide, looping circles. I suppose you could say that they—these ideal readers—keep me in line.

My Third Ideal Reader

This reader is perhaps the most elusive of all. He's an exceedingly picky reader, that's for sure. He's bored easily. He's rarely satisfied with what I've written. He's certainly more pervasive. That's right ... it's *me*.

In short, I would like to write books that I would like to read. I'm constantly asking myself, as I'm writing a story or a novel (especially a novel), if I would keep reading what I've written if I hadn't written it. The good thing about me being one of my ideal readers is that it keeps me honest. It keeps me from cynically writing a book with the marketplace in mind. I write what I would want to read. Should what I want to read, what I'm writing, and the marketplace all converge . . . terrific! But I'm not going to force a book into being more commercial for the sake of writing a commercial book. If I did, I would be bound to fail. The *bad* thing about me being my own ideal reader is that I still haven't hit the bull's-eye. I would love, for instance, to write a book as big and strange and confident as John Irving's *The World According to Garp*. I don't want to write *like* John Irving, but I would love to write a novel that's as brimming with life, as visceral, and as sweeping as *Garp*. Have I done so? No. Will I ever do so? I don't know. And so I continue disappointing this particular ideal reader. I'm not sure if I could ever live up to my ideal reader's expectations, but I don't think that's necessarily a bad thing. It's what keeps me going.

Maybe next time, I tell myself. *Maybe next time.*

EXERCISES

1. Write a very short story (no longer than five pages) with your best friend in mind as its ideal reader. Now, go back and edit the story for a parent. How has the story changed? In what ways did you self-censor? Did this censorship help the story or take away from it?

2. Who wouldn't normally be your ideal reader? Why wouldn't this person be your ideal reader? Write a very short story (five pages maximum) with this person—your anti-ideal reader—as your ideal reader. Afterward, ruminate on how your writing changed. Were there any benefits?

3. Give a public reading of your story. Was there anything you wanted to change as you were reading? If you had to read it again, would you change anything? If not, why not? If so, why?

Subject Matter

I N HIS TERRIFIC BOOK *Making Shapely Fiction*, the late Jerome Stern has a section titled "A Cautionary Interlude," in which he lists different kinds of plots that writers should avoid writing. It's a smart list that illuminates a host of common problems, and I have read that list aloud to my students countless times. In this chapter, I hope to take Stern's idea one step further by listing actual, very specific subjects that carry with them assorted problematic baggage if the writer isn't careful.

Throughout this book I make note of "default modes," by which I mean that beginning writers tend to gravitate toward the same things, whether it's imagery (clichés like "piercing blue eyes"), syntax (overuse of *as he, as she,* or *as they* constructions), or narrative strategies (writing increasingly incomprehensible sentences the deeper a narrator sinks into psychosis). For the experienced reader, the above examples are all painfully familiar—code, if you will, that the person writing the story is either a novice or someone who doesn't listen to criticism of his work. But for the novice writer who is eager to move beyond these default modes, there's no way to know what a default mode is unless the writer reads thousands upon thousands of pages of work by other novice writers, or unless someone with more experience (for example, the creative writing teacher) reveals to the novice precisely what those default modes are.

There are default subject matters, too, and every time I teach a beginning fiction writing course, I can count on seeing many of these at least once. There's nothing inherently wrong with most of these subjects—and, in fact, many great stories have been written using them—but the fact is that most of the stories I read by beginning writers who choose these subjects are not great stories (or even moderately good ones) because each

subject presents one or more potential problems, problems that are difficult to avoid if you don't know what those problems are or why they're
problems.

I'm in a unique position because I have read well over a million pages
of fiction written by beginning writers—frighteningly, this is not an exag-
gerated figure—but also because I have edited theme-based anthologies,
for which I often put out calls for submissions, and what I discovered was
that for every broad subject there's a default story. My first anthology, for
instance, was a collection of stories about adultery. About half of the one
thousand stories I culled through, in my attempt to find a few dozen stories worthy enough to be included in the book, were about older men having affairs with younger women (almost all written by older men), and
most of those were about (surprise!) male bosses having affairs with their
younger female employees. It was hard imagining that these weren't mostly
fantasies recorded for posterity. Most of them were not very good. The
characters were familiar from one story to the next, and the plot arcs were
often predictable. My task was to find the *one good, original version* of this
story. Which story transcended these familiar elements? Which story surprised me?

What this experience taught me was that whenever I sit down to write
my own stories, I need to think carefully about the default version and the
almost insurmountable task of transcending it. If, for instance, I decide
one day to write a father and son story about hunting, I'll need to think
long and hard about all the other father and son hunting stories I've read,
because, let's face it, there are *thousands* of father and son hunting stories
out there. What can I bring to the table that's fresh? What are the tropes
of that particular genre that I need to avoid so that my story doesn't read
like the other two million father-son hunting stories?

In this chapter, I have listed the most common subjects for stories that I
come across each semester in my fiction writing courses, and I've attempted
to explain the inherent pitfalls of each one. Again, I'm not suggesting that
great stories can't be written on these subjects—in fact, I have included for
further reading at least two examples of successful stories and/or novels for

each subject—but since these are default subjects, they lend themselves to becoming familiar, flawed stories.

The Dead Grandmother Story

Substitute grandmother for any family member—although, more often than not, these stories inexplicably feature a grandmother—and you have a story that's being written for every beginning fiction writing course across the country. I suspect most Dead Grandmother Stories are autobiographical and that their authors are writing them for catharsis, but this is also their chief pitfall. The grandmother (or whoever is being eulogized in the story) is almost always a beatific presence, a character that has been airbrushed to perfection.

The structure of these stories is eerily similar in that the main present-time story is of the narrator getting ready to go to the dead person's wake, followed by a scene at the wake itself. These scenes are periodically interrupted by flashbacks: grandma baking cookies; grandma offering pearls of wisdom; grandma's always comforting doughy cheek to press against during the narrator's times of sadness. In these stories, the grandmother is a one-dimensional character, incapable of fault. In other words, she's a character who doesn't exist in real life since no such person actually exists. She's a romanticized fantasy. Sometimes, the grandmother is described as "a typical grandmother," as though such a person exists. My only living grandmother was a miserable soul when I met her. She drank too much and, upon seeing me for the first time, asked me to run an errand for her instead of hugging me or pinching my cheek. She would be my idea of a typical grandmother. See why "typical" doesn't work? It's subjective.

These stories also tend to be steeped in sentimentality in that the language of grief is abstract. The narrator is *sad* or *full of sorrow* or *heartbroken*. The author is expecting the reader to be sad, too, because the narrator is sad, but it doesn't work that way: grief in and of itself isn't interesting. Imagine that you are meeting someone for the first time, and he weeps the entire time you're around him, even though you don't know him at all. Has he earned your sympathy by virtue of the fact that he's crying? (The problem here is that some people are innately sentimental, and they *will* tear up when a stranger reveals that his grandmother has just died, but such behavior isn't the most effective constitution for a fiction writer, who should be earning the reader's sympathy rather than attempting to manipulate it.)

Also in these stories, a lot of attention is paid to tears running down the narrator's face. I call this gratuitous grief. As in movies full of gratuitous sex or violence, the camera, as it were, lingers too long on tears. The author isn't showing restraint. Keep in mind that restraint is more often than not a virtue when writing fiction.

Further reading: William Faulkner's *As I Lay Dying* and Marly Swick's "A Hole in the Language."

The Big Game!

A list of great short stories and novels in which a sport (football, baseball, boxing, etc.) plays a central role would be endless. There are even anthologies of sports fiction. Hell, I even edited one on baseball some years ago. But most novice writers interested in writing a sports story aren't drawing their inspiration from great sports fiction but rather from the game itself or from their own experiences participating in a game. The result is usually a blow-by-blow description of a particular game, with sentences like, "It was fourth and ten, with thirty seconds on the clock. It was now or never, baby! We decided to go for it. No guts, no glory." In other words, these are stories full of tired sports clichés.

Let me state up front that TV *can* do some things better than fiction. Whenever I ask my students which they would rather do, watch a football game on TV or read a blow-by-blow of the same game in a short story, the answer is unanimous: they would rather watch it. This is why such blow-by-blow stories are, among other things, dull. I don't care about what kinds of pass plays are being run, nor do most readers unless they're reading an analysis of a game they just finished watching. But fiction? No one wants to read that stuff. Furthermore, the outcome of such stories is predictable because the team is either going to win, lose, or tie. Ho hum.

So, what makes the great sports short stories and novels great? They are ultimately about people, not an actual game. William Faulkner often remarked that the only subject truly worth writing about was the human heart in conflict with itself. The blow-by-blow stories are often *not* about the human heart in conflict with itself; they're usually about two teams fighting for a championship in which the characters are stick figures moving across a field or court. In the best stories, however, sports is a backdrop that provides, perhaps, a subtext for the plot. Sports is a vehicle for the main character to discover him- or herself not in a cliché way (such a cliché being "I realized that winning wasn't everything"), but rather in a complex, interesting, and fresh way.

Further reading: Ann Packer's "Horse" (basketball), F. X. Toole's *Million Dollar Baby: Stories from the Corner* (boxing), Owen King's "Wonders" (baseball), Patricia Highsmith's "The Barbarians" (baseball), and Leigh Allison Wilson's "Massé" (pool).

Short Stories about Short Stories
(about Short Stories)

John Barth has made a career out of writing stories about stories about stories, sometimes cross-pollinating his own novels and stories, and Barth's work is often brilliant and thought-provoking; but in my beginning fiction writing classes, the story I occasionally see is the story about a main character who can't think of what to write about for his next short story, a story that—you guessed it—needs to be turned in the next day for his short story writing course.

These stories read like free-writing exercises where the writer is spinning his wheels, hoping to gain some traction with a thin idea. The idea almost never works because it's born of either a lack of ideas or self-satisfied cleverness, neither of which results in anything a reader might be interested in reading.

Another problem is that these stories are one-trick ponies. I'm supposed to chuckle over the idea ("Ah ha! A story about a story!"), or my mind is supposed to be blown by the premise ("Holy crap, I didn't see that coming!

Whoa!"), but it usually just elicits a yawn because it's not funny, it's been done before, and I've seen it done better.

Further reading: John Barth's "Lost in the Funhouse" and Tim O'Brien's "How to Tell a True War Story."

The Slice of Life Story

These stories attempt to capture a stretch of time, as though conveying to the reader, "Look, this is how things were for this character in this moment." They are sometimes wonderfully written, too. They remind me, in many ways, of live-action scenes painted on the sides of old buildings. You pause, you admire it, and then you walk on.

These stories, while pleasant enough, often quickly fade from one's mind, probably because there's no reason for their existence. By that, I mean that the Slice of Life Story could have been about any day in the narrator's life. Why is this particular day in the narrator's life any different from another day? In the Slice of Life Story, it isn't. And because it isn't, the story lacks a larger purpose. There's no question being asked or answered, no complication for the narrator to struggle through, no transcendent moment for anyone, including the reader, at the story's end.

There was once a market for these sorts of sketches, but that was sixty, seventy years ago. Editors and readers alike have higher expectations these days for short stories. It's certainly possible to write a story that has slice of life qualities while actually ramping up what's at stake for the main character. Stuart Dybek's "Pet Milk" brilliantly does just that by including the simple insight of the narrator who realizes that he's missing someone he's still with. This awareness gives urgency to the scenes that follow while complicating the narrator's feelings. A potentially erotic scene in the story is shot through with melancholy and desperation instead. In short, this story possesses a reason for being in a way that a true Slice of Life Story simply doesn't.

Further reading: Stuart Dybek's "Pet Milk" and Michael Chabon's "Along the Frontage Road."

The Day in the Life Story

The Day in the Life Story is similar to the Slice of Life Story, except that the author wants to document the main character's entire day, from waking up to taking a shower to getting dressed to eating breakfast to . . . well, you get it.

One of the best delineations between "story" and "plot" can be found in Janet Burroway et al.'s *Writing Fiction*: "A *story* is a series of events recorded in their chronological order. A *plot* is a series of events deliberately arranged so as to reveal their dramatic, thematic, and emotional significance." Therefore, plot is the artistic part of storytelling, the part where the author must make decisions about where to begin, how to order the scenes, how long the scenes should be, and so on. The author of the Day in the Life Story isn't making any choices, except the most obvious: start at the beginning and document everything the narrator does, no matter how trivial. The result is, if I can be honest, a mind-numbingly dull story.

Further reading: James Joyce's *Ulysses*, Sandra Cisneros's "Eleven," and Shirley Jackson's "The Lottery."

The Road Trip Story

The Road Trip Story (or, as I sometimes call it, the One Damned Thing After Another Story) is as American as John Cougar Mellencamp (or Johnny Cougar . . . or John Mellencamp). Consider Kerouac's *On the Road*.

When the Road Trip Story doesn't work—and it usually doesn't—it's because its plot is episodic. Plot should be about causation: this happens *because* that happened. One scene should grow organically out of the previous scene. In the episodic Road Trip Story, however, one scene happens and then another scene happens, but there isn't necessarily any causation between the two scenes. For instance, let's say a character goes on a trip in the first scene and gets a flat tire. And then in the second scene, after having fixed the tire, he gets a speeding ticket. And then, in the third scene, a bird shatters his windshield. Did the bird slam into the windshield because he got a speeding ticket? No. Did he get a speeding ticket because he'd gotten a flat tire? No. The reason these scenes aren't organic is because they're not growing out of characterization; the events in the story are happening because the author is overtly throwing obstacles in the main character's way, but in this sort of plot, anything can happen. A stampede of elephants could run in front of the car, stepping on its hood. A parachuting nun could fall from the sky and land on the roof. A miscreant could drop a bowling ball off an overpass so that the ball lands in front of the car, causing it to swerve into a semi, and then . . . BOOM! The car explodes.

You see how fun it is? And how ridiculous? And how nonsensical?

Further reading: Lauren Groff's "Delicate Edible Birds," Flannery O'Connor's "A Good Man Is Hard to Find," Mona Simpson's *Anywhere but Here*, Jack Kerouac's *On the Road*, Jesse Lee Kercheval's *Brazil*, and Sherrie Flick's *Reconsidering Happiness*.

The Most Awesome Party Story

Write what you know, right?

Many of my undergraduate students have an intimate knowledge of awesome parties. *Crazy* parties. Parties where *insane things happened*. Parties that would make for a *kick-ass* short story!

Whoa. Hold on. Some stories are better told than written. Some stories have a shelf life of twenty-four hours. And some stories have more appeal to your immediate friends than to a broader audience. Think long and hard before you sit down to immortalize your oh-so-awesome party. Ask yourself this: why would anyone care?

This story is similar to cinéma vérité in that the author tries to capture accurately everything for the reader: every drink downed, the slurred words and spinning room, the copious vomit. While I appreciate the author's attempt to be both thorough and visual, the stories have little more purpose than a journal entry. Often, there are too many characters for a writer to do any one character justice; the characters are a cast of interchangeable names who move in and out of scenes.

Further reading: Susan Minot's "Sparks," Valerie Laken's "Map of the City," and Dan Chaon's "Fraternity."

The Victim Story

The Victim Story is one where the main character is continually victim-
ized, often brutally, throughout the narrative. The reader never really gets
a glimpse of this character as anything other than a victim. Oftentimes, the
victimizer is a stock villain—the drunk wife-beater, the always-predatory
(and leering) pedophile, the over-the-top bully. In real life, these are all reprehensible people . . . but they are still people, not types, people who watch
Gilligan's Island reruns or eat their hamburgers without the pickle or own
dogs named Flatt and Scruggs. And from a reader's perspective, it's not interesting to read about someone who is always a victim, because the victim
position is a passive position, a person to whom things happen rather than
a person who makes things happen.

Further reading: Dorothy Allison's *Bastard out of Carolina*, Madison
Smartt Bell's "Customs of the Country" and Stanley Elkin's "A Poetics
for Bullies."

Main Character: Killed!

There was one semester that I grew increasingly depressed after each workshop because my students kept killing off their main characters at the end
of their stories, and the more I kept saying, "no, no, no," the more dead main
characters I would see. My problem with this story is that it's too easy. You
might as well just kill off every main character in every novel or story ever
written. Holden Caulfield gets shot by D. B. and dies. Huck Finn falls off
the raft and drowns. If the ending of a story is supposed to be surprising yet
inevitable—and I happen to believe that's a pretty good ending to aim
for—most stories I read that end in the death of a main character are surprising but not inevitable.

Actually, I do blame J. D. Salinger in part, because of his short story
"A Perfect Day for Bananafish," which ends in a surprise death. I've had
students cite this story as justification for their own surprising deaths in
their stories. Fair enough. But it's just not surprising anymore. What was
once original is now hackneyed. Furthermore, Salinger already did it, so
why repeat it?

This isn't to say that you can't ever have a main character die in a story, but the death should be a fabric of the story as a whole. The much-anthologized story "White Angel" by Michael Cunningham ends with a death, but there are two important things to keep in mind: we are told at the beginning of the story that the narrator's brother is going to die (thereby diffusing a potentially cheap ending) and while the death is of a major character, he's not the main character.

Further reading: Michael Cunningham's "White Angel," Joyce Carol Oates's "Where Are You Going, Where Have You Been?" and Flannery O'Connor's "A Good Man Is Hard to Find."

Surprise!

Stories with surprise endings can be wonderful if the surprise is an organic part of the story. As noted above, the maxim about story endings is that they should be surprising yet inevitable. All too often, I read stories with endings that are surprising but not inevitable. In these stories, the surprise is often the result of withheld information. By that, I mean that the information being withheld is something the narrator would know. Therefore, the author is withholding information for the sake of surprising the reader.

There are numerous problems with this plot. The first is that it defies point-of-view logic. If the narrator knows something important, so should the reader. Otherwise, the author is being overtly manipulative in a cheap way.

Secondly, if the entire story has been building to this surprise, it must not be much of a story. Chances are what's been sacrificed is character development, which may well be the most important aspect of the literary short story: a deep understanding of a character's motivation, an attempt to understand why a character does the things he or she does.

Thirdly, these sorts of stories are as enduring as a joke, which is to say that it may be entertaining once, to someone, somewhere, but it's unlikely anyone will want to read it again, just as someone is unlikely to want to hear the same joke two times in a row. Once you know the punch line, why bother? In a story with an earned ending that doesn't rely on a surprise, the reader should be able to get something new out of it each time she reads it.

Further reading: Margaret Atwood's "Hairball" and Dan Chaon's *Await Your Reply*.

The I'm a Lunatic but Don't Know It Story

The I'm a Lunatic but Don't Know It is a subset of the Surprise! Story. Oftentimes in this story, the reader doesn't realize a character to whom the narrator is speaking is a hallucination or that the narrator's memories are delusions—that is, until a psychiatrist shows up to see how the narrator is doing, saying things like, "Now, you haven't been getting any more, um, *visits* from Lucille, have you?" It's at this point that the reader is supposed to think, *Wait a minute, he was just talking to Lucille, so . . . whoa, was he hallucinating her, and is he, oh my God, crazy?*

In addition to this premise being a cliché, it's also one where the author's presence in the story, due to the overt manipulation, is overwhelming. I'm not suggesting that people don't have hallucinations, only that the *craziness* in these stories is almost always generic, and times when I've asked the authors directly what the narrator was actually suffering from, they invariably don't know. This is a problem. The author is relying on stock ideas of mental health, which ultimately trivializes the subject. What the author is really going for here isn't an exploration of a character with a particular psychosis but rather the thrill of surprising the reader. The story becomes a game. Unfortunately, the game isn't very interesting for anyone who's spent any time reading literary fiction because it's so familiar and manipulative.

Sylvia Plath's *The Bell Jar* and Richard Yates's *Disturbing the Peace*—both of which deal with mental illness—smack of authenticity and honesty. The fact that both authors actually suffered from the things they wrote about may explain why they didn't resort to cheap gimmicks. (See the chapter "The Imitative Fallacy" for a longer discussion.)

Further reading: Sylvia Plath's *The Bell Jar*, John Wray's *Lowboy*, and Richard Yates's *Disturbing the Peace*.

But . . . It's All True!

These stories are steeped in autobiography, and the author uses that convenient crutch to lean on if the characters are thinly written stereotypes or the situation implausibly presented. "But this really happened," the author will say. Well, sorry, but that's not good enough. The fact that something happened doesn't mean that the story you've written is credible or structured in a way that's satisfying for a reader of fiction. Readers have certain expectations based on the genre they're reading. Expectations were, in large part, the real issue behind the James "A Million Little Pieces" Frey scandal. He presented his book as one thing—a memoir—when, in fact, it was really autobiographical fiction. Have you ever taken a sip of milk when you think you're going to sip Coke? It's a rude awakening, let me tell you. If what you're writing is autobiographical fiction, keep in mind that "autobiography" is modifying the word "fiction," which suggests that the criteria of fiction writing is still the most important criteria.

Further reading: Kay Boyle's *Year before Last*, Frederick Exley's *A Fan's Notes*, and Mona Simpson's *Anywhere but Here*.

The Serial Killer Story

Stories featuring serial killers tend to read like treatments for TV shows, focusing more on the sensational aspects of plot rather than the more subtle nuances of characterization. The primary sin of these stories is melodrama, which is the overt manipulation of plot so as to *thrill* the reader. More often than not, it's not thrilling; it's cheesy.

Strong stories featuring killers focus on characterization; they subvert our notions of what constitutes a typical Serial Killer Story. In Joyce Carol Oates's "Where Are You Going, Where Have You Been?"—one of the most chilling stories I've ever read—Oates creates an ominous scenario by slowly (very slowly) taking us through the narrator's realization that her life is in peril. But it's so subtle, and we (as readers) are only a few steps ahead of Connie, the story's teenage protagonist. The author's subtlety is what makes this story haunting. (Subtlety doesn't mean withholding information the narrator knows. Remember: suspense is created by what the reader knows, not by what's withheld.)

Further reading: Richard Bausch's "Spirits," Tom McNeely's "Sheep," and Joyce Carol Oates's "Where Are You Going, Where Have You Been?"

The Shaggy Dog Story

The origin of the phrase "shaggy dog story" is in dispute, but the gist of it is that a dog is described to a group of people as being very shaggy, and the emphasis on the dog's shagginess is heightened with each description, but when the dog is finally revealed, everyone sees that it's actually not particularly shaggy at all. The premise of the contemporary Shaggy Dog Story is based on the narrator's misunderstanding of something he or she's been told, or the narrator's false perception of events, or a gap of information that the narrator doesn't learn until the story's end. There are endless permutations of this plot, the common denominator being that the narrator is missing some important piece of information that is later revealed, bringing clarity to the situation. It's an inherently flawed story, and whenever I run across one, I rarely can think of a way to fix it.

While it's true in real life that we sometimes make decisions based on something we misheard or an incomplete set of facts, such actions seem contrived in fiction. These stories, as a result, lack the emotional kick that a good short story can provide. The reader often thinks, *so what?* when he reaches the end of the story for the simple reason that the resolution didn't grow out of characterization; it grew out of a plot contrivance.

In Richard Russo's "The Whore's Child," Sister Ursula, one of the major characters, experiences a significant misinterpretation throughout most of the short story, but this character is not the narrator, which helps Russo sidestep many of the problems above. Furthermore, the astute reader will be able to piece together the truth of the situation before Sister Ursula does, which means that the story doesn't rely entirely on the revelation of this misunderstanding alone. Finally, the narrator has his own problems, and while those problems constitute less real estate in the story, they are not based on a misunderstanding, even though he's in denial of them. "The Whore's Child" is a very rare story, however, for which a shaggy dog plot actually works.

Further reading: "The Whore's Child" by Richard Russo and "Araby" by James Joyce.

- -

FINALLY, THERE ARE three types of stories I regularly see that usually don't work because of their technique, not because of subject matter.

The Hearsay Story

In these stories, a character—usually the narrator—begins to tell a story that ends up becoming the main story. It's as though there's a story inside of a story: the main story starring our narrator and then the story that the narrator is telling. But the story being told isn't dramatically interesting because it's primarily summarized. Therefore, the reader ends up feeling as though he's sitting across from someone telling a story rather than being a participant in the story. In real life, the person telling us a story may be animated enough to keep your interest, but such animation doesn't carry over to the page.

Whenever I read these stories, I have these questions for the author. Is there a better way to tell the story, perhaps by cutting to a dramatized scene of the story being told to us? Do we even need the person who's telling us the story? Why can't the story being told actually be the story?

Further reading: Lynne Barrett's "One Hippopotamus," Joseph Conrad's *Heart of Darkness*, F. Scott Fitzgerald's *The Great Gatsby*, and Alice Munro's "Five Points."

The Omniscient Story

I spend considerable time going over point of view on the very first day of my beginning fiction writing class. When we reach omniscience, I talk about how it's a point of view that isn't used much anymore and when it *is*, it tends to be used in the form of limited omniscience, which, in short, means that the narrator's voice resembles that of an omniscient narrator but the author limits herself to only one character's consciousness. My most important point is that omniscience—true omniscience that can float from the head of one character to another and possesses an overarching voice for the narration (think of any third person novel by Charles Dickens; think of Tolstoy's *Anna Karenina* or *War and Peace*)—is really best suited for longer works. In a shorter work, the story loses focus with each switch of point of view until the reader isn't sure whose story it really is or who in the story she should emotionally invest herself in.

The real issue, though, is that most beginning writers attempting omniscience don't understand what omniscience is. To the novice, any change in point of view constitutes omniscience, when, in fact, it doesn't. What it constitutes, more often than not, are careless shifts in point of view. When it fails miserably, the author is shifting point of view for purposes of plot contrivance, conveniently shifting so that we're not privy to something that, had we remained in one point of view, we should be privy to. I have seen stories change point of view several times on a single page. When I ask the writer why it changes, the writer usually doesn't know.

The vast majority of contemporary literary fiction is written in either first person singular ("I") or third person limited ("he" or "she"). In both instances, the point of view remains in one point of view throughout the entire story or, in the case of a novel, chapter. (In a novel, the point of view may shift from chapter to chapter. It should be noted that genre fiction is more flexible when it comes to point of view, and I suspect this is where many of my students, new to literary fiction, get their notions of craft.)

Notice in the recommended reading below that both stories are quite long. Also notice the control these authors exhibit. These are not stories where random, inexplicable shifts of point of view occur.

Further reading: "Merry-Go-Sorry" by Cary Holladay and "A Fish in the Desert" by Luana Monteiro.

The Frame Story

The typical Frame Story opens in the present; the vast majority of the story takes place in the past; the story returns to the present for the ending. Why so many writers are drawn to this structure is a mystery to me, although once you notice it as a pattern, you begin seeing it everywhere, as in the movies *Titanic*, *Double Indemnity*, and *Sunset Boulevard*.

Is it necessary?

Sometimes, yes; most of the time, no. If you're thinking of framing your story, you should ask yourself what the relationship is between the present and the past. The familiarity of the structure is such that editors—and many readers—have grown weary of it, so what are you gaining by doing it? Is what you're gaining enough to overcome reader fatigue?

Recommended reading: Margaret Atwood's "Death by Landscape," Michael Cunningham's "White Angel," and Jean Stafford's "In the Zoo."

- -

THESE STORIES ARE the most universal and, when not done well, the most problematic. I'm sure there are other subject matters that other teachers see with regularity. Where I presently teach, I see several "semester abroad" stories each year, written by students who have just returned from their year abroad. When I taught in Colorado, I saw my share of stories about snowboarders. Every university has its own peculiar default story.

At this point, you may be wondering what's left to write about. The point of this chapter isn't to limit what you can write about but rather to illuminate the most common subjects (and strategies) that attract novice writers, to get you to think outside of these subjects (there are millions of other subjects), and to walk you through the problems born of these subjects so that you can avoid making the same mistakes.

EXERCISES

----

1. Pick one of these subjects for a very short story (no longer than five pages) and write the worst possible version of it, heightening all of the pitfalls I've listed. Then write a version that transcends all of these problems, a story that's fresh and pumps new life into an otherwise tired subject.

2. Make a list of movies that fall into the categories I've covered in this chapter. Why do they make good movies—perhaps they're not actually good *good* movies but rather good *bad* movies—but wouldn't work as short stories? Or could any of them have worked as a short story? If so, why?

3. Imagine a bad version of one of the story categories from this chapter. Now, imagine a potential character on the periphery of the story. Let's say he's the mechanic in the Road Trip Story. Or she's the serial killer's next door neighbor who knew nothing about her neighbor until he was arrested. Try writing a story from one of their points of view. Still, you'll want to make sure the story doesn't fall into one of the fatal categories.

Beginnings

THE FICTION-WRITING COURSES I teach should probably be called "The Art of Manipulation" since what the student is graded on at the end of the semester is, in large part, her skill as a manipulator. It's as simple—and as difficult—as that. There are countless aspects of craft that go into the making of a piece of fiction, and yet most of us, myself included, will launch into the writing of a short story without much thought about what the hell we're doing. A sentence may come to us out of the blue, or maybe a fully-formed character, or a line of dialogue, and off we go! Only later do we realize that we've established the ground rules for the story in those first few sentences, and only then do we begin to see how we've limited our opportunities or, if we're lucky, freed ourselves.

According to my first writing professor in graduate school, the late Frank Conroy, the beginning of a short story contains an implied contract that the author makes with the reader. How can I tell when an author has violated this contract? It's simple. One minute I'm reading; the next, I'm ticked off. If it's a published story, I'll toss it aside. If it's a student's story, I'll circle where I believe the contract was broken and put my comments in the margin.

The reader/writer contract in a novel, as opposed to a short story, tends to be established at the beginning of each chapter, which is why you're likely to read books that do, in fact, change voice, style, or even point of view throughout. Some longer short stories or novellas may change voice, style, and point of view, too, but usually the author has broken the story into sections or even micro-chapters. In such instances, the author has carefully prepared the reader to read the story a certain way. The section breaks are like posted warning signs that the rules might change.

The contract varies from story to story, but on the first page, sometimes even the first sentence, the author establishes the story's tone, voice, style, and point of view. The contract requires that these elements remain consistent throughout the story.

Consider "tone." Let's say an author has written a humorous story about an Italian American family, in which the vast majority of the humor grows out of honest, believable situations. Therefore, the humor is primarily organic; it is part of the characters' lives. Now, let's say on page eleven that a son and father get into an argument, and the next morning the son finds the head of a horse in his bed. The reader wonders, *What the hell just happened?*

This is an extreme example of a violation of the story's contract, but I hope my point is obvious: the author parodied a scene from *The Godfather*, and the humor shifted abruptly from organic to authorial. By authorial, I mean that the author's hand entered the story to insert a comic moment that's inconsistent with the rest of the humor. Hence, the violation.

I don't want to belabor the necessity for internal consistency for each story element, but the same is true for voice, style, and point of view. An example of a violation of style might be a story whose first half reads like Hemingway (spare prose that employs a simple syntax) and whose second half reads like Faulkner (lush prose with syntax that bends and twists). Unless there's some logical reason for the switch in style, readers are likely to feel confused or, worse, angry.

Perhaps the primary benefit to sticking with the contract is that the reader won't be jarred out of the story, that the story will maintain what John Gardner called the vivid and continuous dream. Sure, you can break all the rules you want, but it's the rare occasion, in my experience, that a broken rule results in greater gains than losses. Such stories usually accomplish little more than being a showcase for a writer to yell, "Look, I broke all the rules!" as if no one in the long history of writing had ever thought to break the rules. Trust me: there's nothing duller than reading a story that breaks rules for the sake of breaking rules.

THE BEGINNING OF EACH story also establishes psychic distance. Psychic distance—a concept briefly introduced in John Gardner's *The Art of Fiction*—may be defined as the distance that the reader feels toward the story's narrator. The reader may feel very far away, very close, or somewhere in between. As Gardner notes, the difference between the novice writer and the professional writer is how one *controls* psychic distance.

Imagine each sentence below as the opening of a short story. Sentence 1 is an example of the greatest psychic distance the reader feels. Each subsequent sentence brings the reader closer to the point of view of the narrator. As the psychic distance moves closer, the narrator's internal thoughts become more prevalent.

1. **It is August 4, 1977.**
   This sentence is pure exposition. There is no character, no precise setting, only information. The reader attaches herself to a sentence such as this one almost entirely on an intellectual level. If the reader happens to respond on an emotional level, it's because of some personal connection to August 4, 1977, not because of some emotionally resonant moment in the story.

2. **It is August 4, 1977, and it's snowing.**
   In this sentence, which is still mostly expository, we now have a concrete detail: snow. But the snow is disconnected from character or place. We have, at best, a vague image and, perhaps, a mood, although the mood we superimpose is most likely based on how we feel about snow or some memory attached to snow.

3. **A large man walks out of a restaurant and into the snowy night.**
   If you think of this sentence in terms of a movie, it might be the opening shot, perhaps a bird's-eye view of the scene, filmed from

a helicopter. Neither the man nor the restaurant is specific. The details are vague, but at least we now have character and place, even though, in terms of psychic distance, we feel quite distant from them.

4. **Joe Worthington steps out of the Sunset Bar and Grill and shivers.**
Aha! Now we have specifics. These specifics, in turn, begin to give the reader a sense of personality and place. The Sunset Bar and Grill has more character than a "restaurant." As a result, the reader starts feeling closer to the scene. Keep in mind: we are privy only to the external world of the story.

5. **Joe Worthington, thinking about how horribly cold it is outside, steps out of the Sunset Bar and Grill.**
For the first time, the reader is privy to Joe's internal thoughts when he thinks about how horribly cold it is outside. This is significant because the reader can now hook into a consciousness. The fictional world is no longer viewed objectively; it is being filtered, at least in part, through Joe's point of view.

6. **Joe Worthington, stepping out of the Sunset Bar and Grill, thinks about how horribly cold it is.**
On the surface, this sentence doesn't appear much different from the sentence above, but on closer inspection you'll see that the internal thought is now the main clause whereas the action (the external world of the story) is a subordinate clause. Therefore, we are now even deeper inside Joe's head than we were in the previous example.

7. *Damn, it's cold*, **Joe Worthington thinks, stepping out of the Sunset Bar and Grill.**
The difference between sentence 7 and the preceding two sentences is that the reader is now privy to Joe's direct internal thought. We are more fully inside his head. We are probably

more likely to have a visceral response to what Joe thinks and what he does.

8. *Damn, it's cold!*

In terms of psychic distance, this is as close as we can get. We are directly inside Joe's head. In sentence 7 above, we still feel the presence of the author who provides "Joe Worthington thinks." Not here. If the story were to continue in this vein, we'd call it "internal monologue." The external world of the story has entirely vanished.

The issue here isn't whether a close psychic distance is better than a more distant psychic distance. The issues are two-fold. How well does the author control shifts in psychic distance, and is the author using psychic distance to the story's best advantage?

As for control, John Gardner insisted that you shouldn't jump around from, say, sentence 8 to 1 to 7 to 2, and so on. The reader would never feel grounded. Furthermore, the tone of the story would be all over the map. Imagine a movie that jumps from an intense close-up to a bird's-eye view to a medium shot for no logical reason. You'd be so distracted by the randomness of the filmmaker's decisions that you'd have a difficult time paying attention to the story, let alone feeling anything for the story's characters. The same is true for fiction. Control instills confidence in the reader.

Perhaps the chief effect that psychic distance has on a story or novel is tone. Consider the differences between Ernest Hemingway and William Faulkner. Hemingway wrote in a removed psychic distance, which gives the reader the feel of reportage, a kind of objectivity, possibly even a cold detachment to the story's events. Faulkner, on the other hand, wrote in a close psychic distance, so deep inside a character's head that the reader is sometimes disoriented, unsure what's happening in the character's tangible world. The result here is, at times, claustrophobic, intense, and, given the onslaught of internal thought, the prose is lush—pretty much the opposite of Hemingway's. I've chosen these two extreme examples to illustrate the tonal differences that result from vastly different uses of psychic distance.

Psychic distance can also be used to good effect when the writer fears she might be sentimental, which should be avoided. Sentimental prose is usually littered with abstract words conveying a narrator's emotional state, and much of this language comes about because the author has dipped too far into the narrator's head during an emotionally fraught moment. But what if the author decides instead to move out of the character's head and force herself to write from a more removed psychic distance? This would force the writer to focus more on what's actually happening rather than what the narrator is feeling, which we probably know already anyway through inference.

The flipside of sentimentality is melodrama, which is often characterized by too much description of over-the-top actions: explosions, car chases, gore. To counter this, the writer may want to move to a closer psychic distance. Instead of describing pages and pages of a car chase, what precisely is going through a narrator's head as he swerves to miss a school bus? What if he's wondering if he turned the oven off, and then what if he's wondering *why* he's wondering at that particular moment if he turned the oven off? How many times have you heard someone say that they could relate to the main character? Well, this is how you do it. Not all of us have been in a car chase, but we've all wondered if we've turned off an appliance, and so by juxtaposing these two things—the melodramatic action with the familiar internal thought—the writer is subverting melodrama while making us relate to the narrator. Even a monstrous narrator is likely to have thoughts all of us can relate to. The trick to manipulating psychic distance, therefore, is in knowing when to move in closer and when to pull back.

THERE IS PERHAPS no decision in your story you'll make that's more important than point of view. The choices you make in the first sentence will affect the rest of the story. For me, stories often start with character, but sometimes they begin with a haunting image that leads to character development. My story "The New Year" was one such story, but the haunting image I wanted to include wasn't going to appear until near the story's end. So, how was I going to tell this character's story? What was the best point of view?

I wrote the first draft of "The New Year" quickly. It was the first story I wrote where I was hyperconscious of establishing a particular contract with the reader—a contract I found helpful because it allowed me to achieve certain things later in the story. Here are the first three paragraphs —the contract, as it were:

> At midnight, party horns blow obscenely, strangers kiss with tongues, and champagne corks fire perilously across the smoky room like a barrage of SCUD missiles. No one here has ever heard of "Auld Lang Syne," so what they do instead to celebrate the new year is blast the first few tracks off Ozzy Osbourne's *Blizzard of Ozz*.
>
> Two hours later, half the people have gone home, fearing the approaching snowstorm. The remaining half have coupled, staking out for themselves every bedroom, hallway, and closet in the house. Here and there, men and women copulate—some, discretely; others as if auditioning for the role in a slasher film: lots of panting, then moans, then a high-pitched squeal followed by a howl or scream, then nothing at all.
>
> *Dead*, Gary thinks.

I don't introduce any specific characters in the first two paragraphs. The point of view in these paragraphs comes from some authorial voice, a voice hovering far above any individual character. What I was trying to do was establish a limited omniscient point of view: *omniscient* because it employs that hovering-far-above voice; *limited* because it never enters the head of more than one character, in this case Gary. It's not until the third paragraph that Gary, the point-of-view character, is introduced, and I dip into his head for an internal thought, a single word: *Dead*. I made a conscious decision to begin the story this way for several reasons.

Gary is the story's main character. He's the one whose perspective we're eventually privy to. The problem is, Gary isn't the brightest guy in the world, far from it, so if the story had been written from an extremely close third person—that is, a point of view strictly limited to Gary's insights and perspective—the story would probably lack a subtext. For me, subtext is the deeper and murkier and most interesting element of a story. Unfortunately, Gary is unable to understand the subtext or the greater meaning of his life. He has only a surface understanding. Therefore, my fear was that without the *omniscience* of the limited omniscient point of view, the story would not rise above the superficial.

Gary is both stoned and drunk. Imagine how insufferable the story would be written entirely from a limited third person—or, worse, an intensely close psychic distance that would read like an internal monologue. The story would be utterly incomprehensible. (See chapter "The Imitative Fallacy.") I can't say if I entirely accomplished this in "The New Year," but early on I wanted to establish a means of narrating events that would allow me to tell Gary's story with lucidity.

Finally, the first paragraph sets the story's tone—mildly ironic and deadpan—which I would have been unable to achieve in limited third person.

Each story a writer writes teaches him a different lesson about craft, and one thing I learned while writing "The New Year" was how the contract I established at the beginning of a story affected everything that followed it, whether or not I, as its writer, was conscious of it. The last sentence of "The New Year" moves from inside Gary's head outward, back to the omniscient voice that began the story. I didn't plan this. There is no way I could have ended this story with its current final sentence had I established a different point of view at the beginning of the story. But since I hadn't planned to end the story with an omniscient voice, the story apparently took on a life of its own. The contract I had established—and understanding that I was establishing a contract with the reader—opened up a larger world by the story's end.

EXERCISES

----

1. Write the first two pages of a short story with a removed psychic distance and then slowly move closer so that, by the end of the second page, the psychic distance is as close as can be. Rewrite it by starting with a mid-level psychic distance that slowly moves closer so that, by the end of the second page, the psychic distance is as close as can be. Finally, rewrite those pages in a psychic distance that is as close as it can be, or one level removed, without moving any further out.

2. Take a story you've already written and rewrite the opening page from the perspective of each character in the story. If there are ten characters in your story, you should have ten different openings. It may prove to be interesting to explore points of view you wouldn't normally consider exploring. In the end, you may stick with your original perspective, but who knows—maybe you'll discover a new story that demands to be written.

3. Remember how I said that the opening of a story is a contract and how that contract establishes the story's various ground rules? Use the same basic story premise, but open it with three different contracts. If it's a serious story, try opening it as a comic story. If you're using really long sentences, try to write it in sentences that contain no more than five words. Be bold in how radically different the contracts are that you choose.

Titles

WHAT MAKES A good book title?

I used to think that using concrete words instead of abstract words was the ticket, and that the reader should be able to walk away with an image in her head, but now I'm not so sure. Concrete words? Possibly. But an image? All evidence points to the contrary.

Some of the most effective titles have been those that sound good but are otherwise incomprehensible. Take *The Catcher in the Rye*. I'm still not sure what a "rye" is. I *should* know but don't. Before *Jurassic Park* became a megahit, how many people knew what "Jurassic" meant, let alone what it meant in connection to the word "park"? (I'm already thinking about writing *Precambrian Park*, in which jellyfish and worms rule the Earth!) Richard Russo's *The Risk Pool* may be an enigmatic title unless you work for State Farm or Allstate. *The Insurance Risk Pool* would have cleared matters up, but notice how much better the former is than the latter, even when we don't necessarily know what the former means. The latter is too spot-on, too clunky. The beauty of all of Russo's book titles is that any one of them would be at home on a movie theater marquee: *Mohawk, Nobody's Fool, Bridge of Sighs*. But *The Insurance Risk Pool*? Nuh-uh. It sounds like the title of a driver's ed film made in the fifties. Amy Tan's *The Joy Luck Club* is another enigmatic title, and I distinctly remember telling someone upon its release, "No one's going to buy a book titled *The Joy Luck Club*." (You see now why I no longer gamble.) And then there's Thomas Pynchon's *Gravity's Rainbow*—a beautiful title, but what the hell does it mean? Sylvia Plath's *The Bell Jar* is also inscrutable, and yet, like the name of a car, no one questions it. (What exactly is a Corolla, anyway?) The fact that I don't know what in holy hell a matterhorn is hasn't slowed down sales of Karl Marlantes's novel *Matterhorn*, which, as I'm writing this, has been on the *New York Times* bestseller list for many weeks.

You know you've struck gold when everyone shortens your title. John Irving's *The World According to Garp* has become simply *Garp*. Mark Twain's *The Adventures of Huckleberry Finn* has become *Huckleberry Finn* or, better yet, *Huck Finn*. Even a short title like F. Scott Fitzgerald's *The Great Gatsby* is often, simply, *Gatsby*. Unlike their windbag counterparts, women writers have been historically forward-thinking in giving us already-truncated titles. Jane Austen saw no need for *The World According to Emma*, nor did Charlotte Brontë feel the need to present *The Adventures of Jane Eyre*.

Why be original? Some of the best titles have been pilfered from other writers' work: William Faulkner's *The Sound and the Fury* and Ray Bradbury's *Something Wicked this Way Comes* (Shakespeare's *Macbeth*), John Steinbeck's *Of Mice and Men* (Robert Burns's poem "To a Mouse"), Flannery O'Conner's *The Violent Bear It Away* (the Bible; Matthew 11:12), Mark Haddon's *The Curious Incident of the Dog in the Night-Time* ("Silver Blaze," a Sherlock Holmes story by Sir Arthur Conan Doyle). You better start digging through your classics before all the good ones get snapped up.

Charles Simic's *Return to a Place Lit by a Glass of Milk* is a lovely title, one of my favorites, in fact, but it would be a lousy title for a novel. It's perfect for what it is—a volume of poetry. It's no surprise that Delmore Schwartz, whose collection is titled *In Dreams Begin Responsibilities*, was also a poet. Poets tend to want their titles to be, well, poetic. Or, if not poetic, long. Denis Johnson, a trained poet, started off his fiction career with the economically titled novel *Angels*, but a few years down the road he unleashed *Resuscitation of a Hanged Man*.

Some titles haven't stood the test of time as well as others. How could Henry Fielding have known that everyone would eventually think his title *Tom Jones* referred to the Welsh singer best-known for the song "What's New, Pussycat?" Max Frisch's novel *I'm Not Stiller* was fast on its way to becoming a classic, but I'm afraid today's book buyer would pick it up and wonder, "You're not *Ben* Stiller?" Hermann Hesse's novel *Steppenwolf* risked being usurped by "Born to be Wild" band Steppenwolf, who, in point of fact, named themselves after the Hesse novel. My head hurts just thinking about it.

And then, of course, there are those books with extraordinarily long titles I can never remember, like Dave Eggers's *A Heartbreaking Work of Staggering Genius* (I just had to Google it), or Maile Meloy's wonderful collection *Both Ways Is the Only Way I Want It*, which I always refer to as the Journey song, "Anyway You Want It, That's the Way You Need It." I love long titles and wrote an entire story around a title I had wanted to use—"Men Who Love Women Who Love Men Who Kill"—but whenever someone asks me a question about that story, they refer to it as "You know, that story 'Men Who Kill Women,' or something like that."

And what about those title missteps? Did John Sayles shoot himself in the foot titling a novel *Los Gusanos*? Or what about Douglas Unger titling his novel *El Yanqui*? I have nothing against foreign languages, but purely from a marketing standpoint, you run the risk of the American book-buying public thinking that the book itself isn't written in English when the title is in another language. I'm just glad I didn't name my first novel *El Libro de Ralph*.

In all fairness, it doesn't take a foreign title for a book written in English to scare off book buyers. I would be hard-pressed to find a less appealing title for a novel than John Updike's *Memories of the Ford Administration*. Surely more than one person turned quickly away after reading the title. Someone titled their Amazon review of the book "Good News—Not Really about the Ford Administration at All!" Updike isn't alone. I seriously misstepped when I titled my second novel *America's Report Card*. Most people thought I'd written a nonfiction book. Even when I did radio interviews, I was asked about No Child Left Behind and standardized testing in ways that suggested that I was an expert on these subjects rather than a novelist who made crap up. I followed *America's Report Card* with the story collection *Ghosts of Chicago* and have since been asked to visit grade schools to read ghost stories to children, this despite the fact that *Ghosts of Chicago* isn't a collection of ghosts stories and certainly not a book for children. I should have anticipated these problems, but oftentimes you don't realize the mess you've stepped into until it's too late.

If you want to play it safe, you could always go with big, sweeping titles that sound like Comp 101 essays, like *War and Peace* (compare and contrast), *Pride and Prejudice* (personal narrative), *Crime and Punishment* (cause and effect) or *The Agony and the Ecstasy* (description), but take note: With one exception (*Pride and Prejudice*), these novels are *huge*. If you're going to have a sweeping title, you probably need a sweeping novel to go with it.

Sadly, some titles don't click with readers. Charles Portis's novel *Masters of Atlantis* should be on everyone's bookshelf, but I can see people's eyes glaze over whenever I tell them the title. "Sure, sure, I'll look into it," they tell me. Doris Lessing's *Re: Colonised Planet 5, Shikasta* fills me with dread before I even open to the first page. And then there are those writers who, despite having an iconic book title in their pocket, seemed to have lost their title mojo. Salinger's *Raise High the Roof Beam, Carpenters* is dreadful. Once you start putting commas in your title, all bets are off.

If you pay close attention, you may notice title trends. For a while, in the early seventies, the gerund title was in vogue. Dan Wakefield led the pack with *Starting Over, Going All the Way*, and *Selling Out*. These days, when I see a gerund title, I'm immediately put off by it, expecting a story full of shaggy-haired pot smokers, bearskin runs, and trysts with co-eds. (Not that there's anything wrong with any of those subjects in and of themselves; the gerund title just makes it all seem so dated is all.) That said, it didn't hurt David Schickler's sales, whose popular 2001 book is titled *Kissing in Manhattan*. (A shout-out to Manhattan probably never hurts sales.)

One wonders if Ayn Rand's *Atlas Shrugged* would have become the behemoth best seller it did if she had stuck with her original title, *The Strike*. Although it didn't sell in its day, *The Great Gatsby* might have suffered a different long-term fate if it had been named *Trimalchio* or *Under the Ash-Heaps and Millionaires*, two of the many titles F. Scott Fitzgerald considered.

Every once in a while a good gimmick title comes along, like Jincy Willett's *Winner of the National Book Award* or Kathy Acker's *Don Quixote* or, better yet, her novel *Great Expectations*. Should a high school student buy the wrong novel, she might be surprised by how sexually explicit Charles Dickens could be. My favorite gimmick title isn't fiction at all; it's Abbie Hoffman's manifesto *Steal This Book*. Even now, over forty years after it was written, some libraries keep this book behind their front desks instead of on their shelves.

In the end, there are no formulas for a good, effective title. There are no tricks, no surefire bets. I've seen books with what I thought were spine-crawling titles make the best seller list. We each have our own quirks for what we like and what we don't like. I happen to like titles with the word "last" in it—don't ask me why—and so I think James Crumley's *The Last Good Kiss* is a particularly beautiful title. My vote for all-time perfect title goes to *One Hundred Years of Solitude* by Gabriel García Márquez. It's a title that suggests the scope of the book, it's aesthetically pleasing to say aloud, and it looks good on the page. Ironically, my favorite title is a translation. The original Spanish title *Cien Años de Soledad*, which is a literal translation, isn't quite as pleasant to my ear because of how the syllables are stressed differently. Silly, I know, but there's something aesthetically pleasing about the way the rhythm of "one hundred" plays off of "solitude," which leads me to think that maybe what we all need is a good translator— in my case, someone good at translating English into English.

EXERCISES

1. Come up with a hundred different titles for one of your short stories. Some should be concrete. Some should be abstract. Some should be an excerpted line from your story. Some should be one word long. Others should be quite long.

2. What are your top ten favorite book or story titles? Why do you like these? Are there any similarities between them?

3. Find a dozen titles. By "find," I mean look in unusual places for phrases or combinations of words that might make good story or

novel titles. On the box for my printer ink, a sentence begins, "If you do not accept these terms…" I like that as a possible short story title: "If You Do Not Accept These Terms." "Like us on Facebook," which appears on a restaurant receipt, doesn't appeal to me, but cutting off "on Facebook" makes the potential title more interesting: "Like Us." For each title you find, be sure to explain where you found it.

The Narrator's Likeability

THINK ABOUT YOUR own experience of meeting someone for the first time: You usually have a gut response, sometimes before the person speaks. And once the person speaks, you unconsciously move forward or take a step back because you're forming lightning fast opinions and judgments. By stepping in, you're inviting this person into your personal space, your world; by stepping back, you're retreating or putting up a barrier between you and this stranger.

A reader's feelings toward a narrator are similarly complex and mysterious. (Remember: the narrator is the character whose perspective we're in. In a story or novel that remains in one character's perspective throughout, the narrator is usually, although not always, the main character. Therefore, much of what I have to say about a narrator holds true as well for the main character.) Perhaps more than any other element of fiction, the narrator elicits strong subjective reactions. In fact, the reader may read a single page—sometimes as little as the opening paragraph—and decide right then and there that she doesn't like the narrator and won't read any more of it. The reader may find the narrator silly, depressing, annoying, pathetic, or dull. If reading a novel or story is a journey, the reader may jump ship shortly after it leaves port and swim back to shore rather than spend the next however-many-days with someone she deems silly, depressing, annoying, etc.

To complicate matters, men and women sometimes respond differently to main characters. In my Humor in American Literature course, several men found the female protagonists of Lorrie Moore's stories to be "whiny." Therefore, they didn't like the stories. The women, however, could "relate" to the protagonists (*relate* is a word that comes up a lot during discussions of main characters) and, therefore, championed the stories. Similarly, I've sat in classes where women have reacted negatively to Ernest Hemingway's main characters, calling them "sentimental," "macho," "jerks." Conversely, male writers often cite Ernest Hemingway as one of their strongest influences. (Of course, I know men who like Lorrie Moore and women who like Ernest Hemingway, but the issue of a reader's gender can't be easily dismissed. There's a reason why, to use extreme examples, readers of Tom Clancy and Clive Cussler are predominantly male while readers of so-called chick lit are predominantly female.)

Reactions to narrators are often personal. You pick up a book, and if the main character reminds you of someone you know and don't like, you'll throw the book down. Or you'll keep reading but find yourself yelling at the narrator: "Stupid! You fool!"

Based on my own experience as a writer, I can say with confidence that no writer can please everyone. It's impossible. I'll read reviews of my work and not even recognize the character they're describing. This holds true for both positive and negative reactions to characters. It may be that the critics are recognizing in one of my characters an aspect of someone they know. It may be that they see aspects of themselves. If readers know something about me and my background, they'll sometimes assume I'm writing about myself even when I'm not. In each instance, the reader is superimposing something over the character that simply isn't there. Sometimes it's something negative, but sometimes it's something positive, and it's this positive superimposition that keeps the reader engaged. But how do you, as a writer, control that? You can't. I've seen a few of my narrators described as losers, narrators whom I thought were honorable but simply dealt a bad hand in life. For all I know, "loser" is the way readers who haven't had bad luck in their own lives view those who can't seem to get things to go their way. As a writer, you put your work out into the world, and then the readers start heaping their own baggage and preconceived notions onto the work, and it's usually the narrator who ends up carrying the brunt of that weight. Unless your work is being read by an audience of robots, it's futile to think you can get everyone to see the narrator precisely as you see him or her.

The Likeable-Likeable Narrator

The point of this chapter—as with many chapters in this book—is to suggest ways of looking at aspects of your story or novel so that you, as author, can consider what you gain and what you lose by the choices you make. I'm not necessarily suggesting that one choice is preferable to the other. As an artist, you'll have to make your own aesthetic judgments. But every choice you make has an effect on the reader. Therefore, I have divided a narrator's likeability into three categories: the Likeable-Likeable Narrator, the Likeable-Unlikeable Narrator, and the Unlikeable-Unlikeable Narrator.

The Likeable-Likeable Narrator is the narrator that we not only enjoy spending time with on the page but would probably feel fondness for in real life as well. This is the all-around decent narrator—flawed, sure, but flawed in a way that most readers can relate to, probably because the reader recognizes those flaws as being her own.

Another way of considering this narrator is in terms of moral ambiguity. While moral ambiguity—that gray area where good and bad intersect and become fuzzy—is a trait of nearly all complex narrators, this particular narrator's gray area is, by and large, on the side of good. It's not surprising, then, that these narrators are often children. Think of Alice Sebold's *The Lovely Bones*, which is narrated from the afterlife by a dead child who has been murdered. Obviously, there are more factors in this example than the narrator's having been a child, but the fact is that children are almost always given the moral benefit of the doubt.

A less dramatic story premise with a child at its core is James Joyce's "Araby," a classic innocence-to-disillusionment story. The subject is love, and how a boy's perception of it changes from a romantic ideal to a more realistic disappointment. There's a pretty good chance that the reader has experienced an arc similar to what the boy in "Araby" experiences, and, as such, we are especially sympathetic to him.

In theory, this narrator has the best chance of reaching the greatest number of readers, if only because it's the narrator that would be the least offensive, but once we start talking about mass appeal, we find ourselves in murky waters since there are thousands of examples to the contrary and especially since there are so many other factors involved, many of which are out of the writer's control.

The Likeable-Unlikeable Narrator

The Likeable-Unlikeable Narrator is someone we enjoy spending time with on the page but probably would steer clear of in real life. In order for this narrator to work, there must be something redemptive about him or her—or, if not redemptive, something charming. Or perhaps it's prurience on our part that makes us stick around. In other words, there's got to be *something*. I would venture to guess that most great literature falls into this category, whether it's Mark Twain's Huck Finn or Flannery O'Connor's Hazel Motes (*Wise Blood*) or, in an extreme case, Vladimir Nabokov's Humbert Humbert (*Lolita*). Yes, a pedophile can be a Likeable-Unlikeable narrator, in this instance due to the beauty of the language (Humbert's narration) and Humbert's, well, irresistible charm.

It's also possible for our feelings toward a narrator to change during the course of the narrative, as mine did for Connie in Joyce Carol Oates's classic story "Where Are You Going, Where Have You Been?" At the story's beginning, Connie is an annoying, self-centered, self-pitying teenage girl. What's to like? From the outset, however, the story itself, the narrative drive, and the language are engaging enough to hook me in. As the story progresses, my sympathies toward Connie grow, not only because I see that she may have had good reasons for behaving the way she did but because of the terrible situation in which she finds herself. Page after page, she becomes an increasingly sympathetic narrator. (This particular story is written in limited omniscience, which means that while we are in Connie's point of view, we are also being fed information from the author's perspective—or, more accurately, the *omniscient narrator's* perspective. This strategy allows us a view of Connie that is simultaneously subjective and objective, which makes her behavior early on more palatable.)

What makes the Likeable-Unlikeable Narrator interesting for many readers is the moral ambiguity, which is to say that the reader is siding with someone they might otherwise dislike or avoid. Whatever redemptive qualities the author has bestowed upon the narrator makes it possible for the reader to buy into the story, as it were, thereby experiencing a world she might not otherwise experience in real life.

The Unlikeable-Unlikeable Narrator

The Unlikeable-Unlikeable Narrator is a tough nut. Frankly, I don't see many published examples, because, let's face it, if the reader doesn't want to spend time with the narrator in real life *or* on the page, the reader is unlikely to buy the book. And if no one wants to buy the book, who's going to publish it? I've read a few published novels with Unlikeable-Unlikeable Narrators, and the only reason I continued to read was because I couldn't believe the book had gotten published. I kept trying to imagine who the audience for it was. And yet, there it was: a published book by a writer with a healthy career of many published books. What I can say about this, from a publishing standpoint, is that this author's work appeals to a niche market, and the publisher must have figured out a way to exploit that niche.

I rarely see these narrators, but occasionally one of my students will turn in a story with an Unlikeable-Unlikeable Narrator, and every once in a while I'll encounter a narrator who's so morally disgusting (racist or sexist, for instance) that I can't find any way into the story as a reader. The main problem with this sort of narrator is that we don't know where the author stands in relation to the material. Is the author also racist or sexist? It's always dangerous to presume a connection between author and narrator, but most writers tip their hand (often subtly) as to what their own moral stance is. However, when that cue is missing—and when the narrator possesses no redeeming characteristic for the reader to grab onto—we can't help but wonder what the author's deal is. So, if the author has written an unredemptive narrator who's also a morally reprehensible person, how does she show the reader that she's not condoning the behavior? And how does she show it in a way that's not didactic?

John Updike subtly pulls this off in "The Lovely Troubled Daughters of Our Old Crowd," a story whose narrator is an older man in town waxing nostalgic about the good old days while wondering what's wrong with the young women who've never left town. What we learn (very subtly) is that his behavior—as well as the behavior of the other parents in town—was damaging to the women when they were girls and teenagers, and yet the narrator remains oblivious to the nature of cause and effect until the very end of the story. But it's here, at the very end of the story, that we see the narrator not so much as a nostalgic old man but for what he really is: a predator. The *reader* is the one whose view of the narrator changes, and the reader's view changes because Updike oh-so-gently tips his hand to us that he, too, sees the narrator's flaws.

I SUPPOSE THERE'S a fourth category, the Unlikeable-Likeable (not to be confused with the Likeable-Unlikeable)—that is, a narrator with whom the reader would like to hang out with in real life but not on the page. I decided against including this one for the simple reason that this narrator is probably the result of poor writing rather than a conscious decision made by the author. To be honest, I can't even imagine what shape or form this character might take, so let's just push this category far from mind. Should I ever see a successful example of this, I'll reconsider my thoughts here, but since I can't fathom one, I'll pretend it doesn't exist.

EXERCISES
----

1. Tweak one of your stories so that there are three different versions: one with the Likeable-Likeable Narrator, one with the Likeable-Unlikeable, and one with the Unlikeable-Unlikeable. Is one version more satisfying to you than the others? Let a trusted reader read all three, and ask for their opinion.
2. Make a list of your narrator's likeable and unlikeable traits. Then switch some of those out. Instead of grumpy, make her cheerful.

Instead of being a murderer, make her a philanthropist. Write the first three pages again but with these new traits. If you like where the story is going, keep writing.

3. Make a list of your own likeable and unlikeable traits. Be honest with yourself. Now, imagine how someone might like your unlikeable traits and dislike your likeable traits. Write a story from that person's perspective.

Minor Characters

THE BREAD LOAF Writers' Conference is the oldest writing conference in the country. Suggested by Robert Frost and founded in 1926, the conference is an institution in American letters, an eleven-day orgy of, among other things, poetry and fiction workshops and readings. The readings by both novice and well-known writers are held twice daily inside the Little Theater, a large barn with bleacher seating.

I attended the conference in August of 1999, and on the night that esteemed poet Ed Hirsch was to read, nearly all of the seats in the Little Theater were taken. I was sitting in one of the top bleachers at the far back of the theater with a few of my new friends. Gathered in the row in front of us were the Bread Loaf fellows—writers fresh with their first published books, a handsome group of men and women with nothing but the promise of more fortunes ahead of them. In short, the envy of Bread Loaf.

As is the case at most poetry readings, the audience responded to Ed Hirsch's work with soft grunts of affirmation, the usual "oooooo"s and "ahhhhh"s, and the appreciative head bobbing. Then, during a moment of silence, a pregnant pause between stanzas in one of Hirsch's poems, my new friend D. G. leaned sideways and let rip the loudest fart I'd ever heard. To give some seismographic sense of its magnitude, I need to take you, dear reader, outside of the Little Theater, where D. G.'s friend Michael was stationed. Michael was smoking a cigarette and waiting for the reading to end. He was several hundred feet away, a wall separated him from us, and yet he clearly heard the resounding blast, too. Not only did he hear it, but he had his suspicions as to who was responsible. For a man *outside* to have heard it, you can only imagine the shock and disgust *inside* the theater. Several dozen people had turned around, hoping to catch the offender. The only person, it seemed, who didn't hear it was Ed Hirsch, the poet. Without missing a beat, Hirsch carried on with his poem, reading the next stanza.

I was thirty-three years old that year, my title at the conference was "scholar," and yet it took all my willpower not to start laughing. I stared Zen-like out of one of the barn's windows, into the Vermont darkness, emptying my head of all thought; but then I caught D. G.'s reflection in the window, his face contorted from holding back his own laugh, and then I heard him snort, and I couldn't help it: I snorted in return. A fiction fellow in the row in front of us turned around to shoot D. G. a look, but a wave of fumes must have hit her entire row at that exact moment, and all the fellows, including a future Pulitzer Prize winner, pitched forward. One of them even gagged.

Months later, D. G. sent an e-mail to me. He signed it, "The Boy That Had Created the Disturbance at the Ed Hirsch reading."

Edgar Marsalla, in the words of Holden Caulfield, is "the boy that had created the disturbance" in J. D. Salinger's *The Catcher in the Rye*. Marsalla was sitting in the row in front of Caulfield in the chapel, and during a speech by one of the school's donors, Marsalla "laid this terrific fart" that "damn near blew the roof off."

"It was a very crude thing to do, in chapel and all," Caulfield says, "but it was also quite amusing."

But after damn near blowing the roof off with his terrific fart, Edgar Marsalla never returns to *The Catcher in the Rye*. He enters the book, creates a scene, then leaves—the fate of many minor characters.

In his book *Aspects of the Novel*, E. M. Forster discusses what he calls flat characters. He writes, "Flat characters were called 'humours' in the seventeenth century, and are sometimes called types, and sometimes caricatures. In their purest form, they are constructed round a single idea or quality."

Our days and nights are crowded with flat characters—people who, like Edgar Marsalla, enter our lives, make a scene, and then leave—but it's the scene they make, large or small, that we remember them by, and by which we define them. (I did not know D. G. before Bread Loaf, and if I had never seen him again afterward, I would always think of him bent over at that Ed

Hirsch reading, red-faced and snorting, actually convulsing from trying not to laugh—the perennial grade school prankster.)

Salinger was a master at the minor (or flat) character, and *The Catcher in the Rye* is full to bursting with these folk. There are over fifty-five such characters in the novel, many of whom never appear again; many of whom, in fact, never actually appear in real time in the book at all, floating ghost-like through the dark recesses of Holden Caulfield's mind. If they *do* appear, they do so as bit players, characters of little or no long-lasting consequence to Holden or the novel's plot. And yet without these minor or flat characters, *The Catcher in the Rye* would evaporate in our hands. *Poof.* No more book. To excise these minor characters would be a literary massacre, for what we have in *The Catcher in the Rye* is an entire population of them.

My own copy of *The Catcher in the Rye* is a beat-to-hell hardback in its sixty-third printing, an ex-library copy with a protective Mylar cover. Reading the book once again, I placed yellow Post-it notes at the introduction of each minor character, and by the time I finished reading it, the book had become bloated with yellow stickies, names and attributes curling into view. It was as though the book had become a tenement and the characters were peeking out from its pages.

Salinger uses characters the way a pointillist uses paint: Stand back, and you'll see a portrait of Holden Caulfield. But it's more than that, really, because the *way* that Holden sees these characters says a lot more about Holden Caulfield than it says about any individual character, the cumulative effect of which is that we see, by the end of the novel, not only a portrait of Holden but a blueprint of his psyche as well, his vision of the world.

For my money, this is the beauty of the book. There's much to be said about the *voice* of the novel, but frankly the voice gets old in places, and Holden's tics (all of his "and all"s at the end of sentences, or calling everyone "old" so-and-so) start to grate on me, especially once Salinger starts piling them on, sentence after sentence. These tics become a literary affectation, a device to *create* Holden's voice, but devices in and of themselves often call too much attention to the creator. The minor characters, however, are gems that don't linger on the scene long enough to grow stale.

There are so damn many characters in *The Catcher in the Rye* that the book becomes a profile of personality prototypes, but what makes the characters unique isn't a set of abstract characteristics. More often than not, Salinger provides us with a gesture, and it's this gesture that pumps blood into the heart of the character, bringing him or her to life. The gesture is so precise, so *perfect*, that we recognize it—we know what sort of person would behave this way—and it becomes difficult to read the novel without matching Salinger's characters to real people we know.

When I read about Ackley, the kid who lives in the room next to Holden's at Pencey, and how when he's done looking at the photo of Sally Hayes he puts it back in the wrong place, I can't help but to remember similar people from my own life, people who pathologically put things back in the wrong place—books on shelves, in particular. These people, they're all Ackley, each and every one of them. Holden says, "He did it on purpose. You could tell." Yes: You *could* tell. Absolutely. Holden's right.

Even when Holden offers a sweeping generalization about a group of people, the generalization is so fresh and acute that it quickly gloms onto the face of a flesh-and-blood person—one of the many minor characters from our own lives—and then through an act of literary transference, that group takes on a distinct personality and becomes a minor character in its own right, albeit a *cumulative* minor character. Early in the novel Holden says of Pencey, "The more expensive a school is, the more crooks it has—I'm not kidding." One of the biggest crooks I ever knew was a graduate of one of the most expensive universities in the country, and after Holden draws this connection for me, I begin to populate the Pencey quad, its dormitories, and its classrooms with this mumbling, snickering guy I once knew. Okay, for the record, he wasn't the *biggest* crook I've known, not by a long shot, but he was certainly the most consistent and most annoying, in large part because he had come from a family with money and because most of what he did was so petty you ended up feeling guilty calling him out on it. Once, while standing in front of a parking meter, he asked me for a quarter, and after I gave it to him, he stuffed it into his pocket and then started walking away from the meter, striking up a conversation so that I would forget he'd just taken my quarter. Or he'd eat with me at a restaurant and then leave just before the waiter delivered the bill. Or he'd try to pay for his beer with the tip I had left for the bartender. Or he'd steal books from my house, tucking them under his coat when I wasn't in the same room.

What I'm saying is this: you know these people. *The Catcher in the Rye* hasn't endured simply because of what's on the page but what we, as readers, bring to those pages. It's exactly what I tell my students *not* to do when they're talking about one another's stories in class—"Don't critique a story based on your own life experiences or how you, personally, could relate to it . . . don't superimpose your own experiences onto the story . . . the story must work on its own, with or without your life experiences. . ."—and yet Salinger causes me, to some extent, to reconsider the issue. After all, isn't that part of Salinger's unique talent, his ability to make the reader say, page after page, "Oh, yeah, I relate to Caulfield," or "I know a guy just like Ackley"? Salinger's genius is his ability to create the universal out of the individual. I didn't go to a prep school, after all. I attended so-so public schools in Chicago-area working-class neighborhoods. On the surface, I have nothing at all in common with Holden and his cast of characters. But it doesn't matter. An Ackley is an Ackley is an Ackley, and I know Salinger's Ackley as well as I know my own Ackley.

Keeping in line with Forster's theory that flat characters are "created round a single idea or quality," Salinger uses the single brushstroke approach to characterization—one sentence, one swipe of his brush, and there you have it. We're given a detail or an action or something that the character says, and it's enough to nail the bastard for good. "That's exactly the kind of guy he was," Holden says of Ernest Morrow, who likes to snap his classmates' asses with wet towels, and with each subsequent brushstroke for each new character, the implication is that *this is the sort of person he or she is.*

- The old, bald bellboy with the comb-over.
- Faith Cavendish, former burlesque stripper, who "wasn't exactly a whore or anything but that didn't mind doing it once in a while."

* The spooky, skinny prostitute named Sunny.
* Dick Slagle, who'd say snotty things about Holden's Mark Cross suitcases but then hope that people thought the suitcases belonged to *him*.
* Louis Shaney, the Catholic kid from Whooton, always looking for an opening to mention the Catholic church in town in order to gauge if Holden was a Catholic, too.
* Sally Hayes's mother who'd do charity work only if "everybody kissed her ass for her when they made a contribution."
* Gertrude Levine, Holden's partner during the museum field trips, whose hands were "always sticky or sweaty or something."
* The woman who cried all through the movie but wouldn't let her own kid go to the bathroom. ("You take some somebody that cries their goddam eyes out over phony stuff in the movies, and nine times out of ten they're mean bastards at heart.")
* Holden's "stupid aunt with halitosis" who kept saying "how peaceful" Allie looked in the coffin.
* James Castle, who wouldn't take back what he said about a conceited kid. (Of course, he jumped out of a window and killed himself, but there you have it: bullheadedness at the expense of everything.)
* Richard Kinsella, whose lip quivered when he made a speech.

We do this when we talk about the minor characters in our own lives—it's the shorthand of characterization—but in spontaneous conversation we're more likely to fumble, throwing out too many defining characteristics, waiting for the light to go on in our listener's eyes. We become Mitchell Sanders from Tim O'Brien's short story "How to Tell a True War Story": "I could tell how desperately Sanders wanted me to believe him, his frustration at not quite getting the details right, not quite pinning down the final and definitive truth." What we're doing is contradictory, really: we want to nail down the single truth about an individual, and yet we want to capture the universality within that individual that will allow our listener to see both at the same time, the specific person we're talking about as well as the *type* of person. This is the Salinger trick of peering at a character through a microscope with one eye while the other eye peers through a telescope.

Logic dictates that if our own lives are filled with minor characters, then we must occasionally play the role of minor character in others' lives. And what sort of minor character are we? What is our single brushstroke? I have to tell you. It's usually not pretty.

Here's a true story. Our family moved around a lot when I was a kid, so I frequently changed schools. In third grade—my first year in what would be my fourth new grammar school in as many years—I had the misfortune of throwing up during class. My stomach took me by surprise, and after I had vomited, I set off a chain reaction among the other weak-stomached students around me. At least three other kids followed suit and vomited, too. A year later, my parents and I moved again—it had nothing to do with me puking—and I attended yet another grade school. Several more years passed, though, before I rejoined my former third-grade classmates in high school, and, sure enough, a guy from that class came up to me one day in the cafeteria and said, "Hey, I remember you. You're the kid who threw up so much that it covered his entire desk."

Was that how everyone remembered me? The Kid Who Vomited So Much It Covered His Entire Desk? Would this be my lasting legacy?

He didn't seem to remember anything else about me except that I was new to that school, that I had voluminously blown chunks, and that I had moved shortly thereafter. No doubt he had worked out his own chain of logic and believed that my leaving the school had to do with my embarrassment, and I have no doubt that after I had moved away he told his theory to anyone who would listen, creating the myth of the Boy Who Vomited So Much It Covered His Entire Desk. Like Holden, this kid was creating his own vision of the world by choosing what (and what *not*) to remember, and his memories, in this instance, certainly said more about him than me.

Here's where real life and fiction part ways. In real life, we are the protagonists of our own ever-unfolding stories. In fiction, we play the role of implied friend to the protagonist, and if I were to write a story titled "The Boy Who Vomited So Much It Covered His Entire Desk," I wouldn't write it from my point of view. No, I'd choose the other kid—a natural protagonist —because he's the one who, if I were the reader, I'd prefer to pal around with. He's the one telling stories, after all. He's the one painting a distinct view of the world (*his* view), and my role in the story was that of the flat character, a minor character in *his* life.

Maybe this is why I don't write heavily autobiographical short stories. Maybe I'm too passive to play the lead. It's true, though, that when I write stories, the character with whom I most relate, nine times out of ten, is the narrator, particularly if my narrator is younger than I happen to be. I relate to them because I hand over to them my best characteristics. *Here, try this on for size.* Or perhaps what I'm doing is giving them characteristics I *wish* I had possessed. As a result, they are more charming than me, more lively, and often funnier. They are like me but not me. They are who I'd *like* to have been. The minor characters in my stories are often the heavies. They, too, can be funny, but frequently they are pathetic or sinister or, well, downright creepy. They are, by and large, a sad lot. They're *not* me. Let me repeat: they are not me.

The fact is, we don't like being minor characters. Rarely when we read do we see ourselves as the minor characters. Everyone relates to Holden Caulfield, but no one says, "Hey, I'm that bald guy with the comb-over!" Or, "Hey, I'm that guy who likes to snap people's asses with towels!" Is it that the real life people who represent these minor characters don't read books and so are never privy to seeing themselves in print? Or is it that they *do* read but see only their heroic side? We're all, each of us, the protagonist, right? We're all David Copperfield, Scout, and Harry Potter. Or is it that when we run across ourselves as flat characters, we *do* recognize ourselves but hope that no one else will? "Okay, sure, I'm the guy who liked to snap people's asses, but surely no one will see *me* in *him*." Are some people inherently inclined to be minor characters in life? Or is it just a matter of point of view: we see the guy with the comb-over, and we think, *Ah, the sad sack . . . the poor bastard,* but in truth the guy with the comb-over has his own triumphs and failures, however large or small, and he is, in fact, no less a minor character than Holden Caulfield, who, after all, is a failure of sorts too and could easily have become a minor character from, say, Ackley's point of view?

And then there's the late J. D. Salinger himself. He's been called a great —if not the greatest—minor writer of the twentieth century. By virtue of his meager output, however, he's relegated himself to literature's minor leagues. But there was the issue of his self-imposed exile, too. Salinger had chosen a path that easily leant itself to pigeonholing by the media (*those phonies!*) and by all those people who devoured what the media spit out about him. Mention Salinger's name to someone who's never read him, who's never been charmed by Holden's voice, who's never met those fifty-plus characters in *The Catcher in the Rye* or any other character in *any* of his books—mention his name, and what are you likely to hear?

Oh, yeah, him, the recluse.

And in a single, sad brushstroke, Salinger himself becomes a minor character, forever playing second fiddle to his own great creation, Holden Caulfield.

EXERCISES

1. Make a long list of minor characters in your life—real people whom you don't know very well—and write a one sentence description (a brushstroke) beside each name. Are any of these characters worthy of making it into your fiction?

2. Take a look at one of your own short stories. Put together a list of all the minor characters in it, along with whatever descriptions you've given them. Which descriptions are weak? Which ones go on too long? Try to replace those with a vivid but succinct sentence, then reinsert them into your story.

3. Make a list of minor characters in one of your stories. What don't you know about each one? Write down some important things that you don't know—what the character does for a living, how old the character is, etc.—then try to fill in the blanks for what you don't know. Is any of this new knowledge worth putting into your story? Now that you know more about your minor characters, are any of them worthy of having their own story?

Immediacy

YOU START READING a book, and without realizing it, you've blocked out everything around you: noises, the room you're in, the people around you. It's classic sensory deprivation, similar to what you experience during a good movie in a dark theater when your attention is fully focused on the screen. You are no longer a mere observer. You've become a participant.

Of course, the opposite can happen, too. If the book isn't effective, if the words on the page are wooden and the story is dull, *everything* will distract you from the page: the fly across the room, a car without a muffler two blocks away, the pattern of the wallpaper, your cuticles.

There are thousands of things beyond the writer's control that may distract a reader from a story or novel (stress, a noisy house, exhaustion), and there are issues, such as profanity, sex, or violence, that may distract the reader based on her own thresholds (my threshold for profanity is quite high). But there are also craft-related issues that may either bring the reader closer to the story or push the reader away, depending upon the author's control of craft. Many of these issues are connected to the concept of *immediacy*.

John Gardner, as I have already noted, wrote that the author's primary obligation was to create the vivid and continuous fictional dream, "captured in language so that other human beings, whenever they feel it, may open his book and dream that dream again." Immediacy is what the writer who accomplishes what Gardner suggests achieves and what, in turn, the reader experiences. Immediacy is that one-to-one ratio of words-to-experience, a transference that may be the most difficult thing for a writer to achieve but one that may make the difference between an effective and an ineffective story. In stories that aren't immediate, the reader feels as though she's reading words on a page, and while she may feel a level of engagement, it's not as much as it should be.

This chapter explores the twenty most common craft-related issues that lessen immediacy for the reader. I've chosen these twenty because they are the ones that come up again and again whenever I've judged a contest or taught a class or read manuscript submissions for a magazine or anthology. These are, in my experience, the worst offenders. Some of these problems are pretty basic, the kinds of problems that a copyeditor's pen could solve, while others are more conceptual and not easily fixed.

Most beginning writers—and many experienced writers while writing their early drafts—write in what I call "default mode" (see the chapter "Subject Matter"). Stories and novels written in default mode look as though they've all been written by the same writer when, of course, they haven't been. The writer writing in default mode is relying on whatever's easiest, whether it's imprecise language or redundant syntax. Almost all of the craft issues that undermine immediacy are a result of default mode writing.

Of course, there are those writers who want you to be aware of their prose, writers whose goals are *not* to create a vivid and continuous fictional dream. In these instances, cleverness and self-conscious prose trump invisibility. But that's not what's under discussion in this chapter. What's under discussion is mimetic fiction: fiction that attempts to capture life without calling attention to the author.

If you are a beginning writer, you should go through this list, determine which of these you're most guilty of committing, and work on those in particular. I'm not afraid to call these a list of rules. I know the cliché, that rules were meant to be broken, and I can think of exceptions to almost all of the rules below, but I suggest you consider these two things before breaking them. One: Think of every craft-related choice you make in terms of cause and effect. If you choose to do "y" instead of "x," you may alienate your reader. If your goal is to alienate your reader, fine. But then you should ask yourself why that's your goal. Two: Don't think you're the first person in the history of the written word to have broken any of these rules. Too often the writers who think they're being edgy and radical are predictable and boring because their goal isn't to tell a good story in the best way possible; it's to take an aesthetic stance, regardless of the fact that the stance has already been taken by hundreds of thousands of fiction writing students (and many professional writers) before them.

Here is the checklist of issues, followed by a discussion of each issue.

* Dialogue Tags That Yell for Attention
* Giving the Verb to the Body Part Instead of the Person
* Redundancies
* Not Cutting to the Sensory Detail Fast Enough
* Favoring Adjectives and Adverbs Instead of Precise Nouns and Verbs
* Simile and Metaphor Overload
* Referring to Memory, Thoughts, Recollections
* Using Authorial Language
* Clichés
* Documenting the Day
* The Curse of Foreshadowing
* Lack of Exposition
* Not Beginning in a Specific Time and Place
* Backstory
* Cramming Too Much into the Container
* Gratuitous Details instead of Details Filtered through a Distinct Consciousness
* Using Weak Sentence Structures
* No Control of Psychic Distance
* A Fixation on Physical Description
* Searching for Substitute Words instead of Using Commonplace Ones

Dialogue Tags That Yell for Attention

The reason given by my students for using words like "queried," "probed," and "verbalized" instead of "said" or "asked" is that they grow tired of using the same words over and over, and they want to find words that are more interesting. My reply is *please, don't!* I understand the impulse to find an original way to write something that seems otherwise mundane and repetitive, but dialogue tags, like punctuation, are conventions and, like periods and quotation marks, tend to remain invisible to the reader unless the writer calls attention to them. Imagine a writer deciding to use smiley-face emoticons instead of periods. How annoying would that be! Or, what if the writer decides to use plus signs instead of quotation marks? The same is true when writers decide that "said" and "asked" are boring. The writer may think he's being original, but the reader starts imagining the writer sitting at his desk with a thesaurus, searching for every possible substitute, whether the new word makes sense or not. Consider this exchange:

"You're joking!" she guffawed.
"No way," he chortled.
"What are you guys talking about?" Mary queried.
"Quiet," Jack hissed.

Whenever I see this sort of thing happening in a story or novel, I skip ahead because I know that the author will eventually run out of verbs for "said" and that the dialogue tags are going to become more and more ludicrous. Even in this short exchange, the dialogue tags are not only silly but inaccurate. How can Jack *hiss* the word "quiet"? There's no "s" in the word, making it impossible to hiss. Tone-wise, this exchange is a disaster. While "guffawed" and "chortled" are of a piece, "queried" is antiquated. You see what's happening? The story—whatever story is here—has been stomped to death by the dialogue tags. Once that happens, the story is no longer immediate. It's just a collection of haphazard words on a page without concern for the effect these words have on the reader.

Giving the Verb to the Body Part
Instead of the Person

Allan Gurganus, one of my workshop teachers in graduate school, pointed out this problem in one of my stories. I call this problem the "disembodied body part acting of its own volition." In these sentences, you'll find eyes rolling, bouncing, and traveling; you'll watch hands grabbing things; you'll see feet leading the way. But where are the people attached to all of these body parts?

> Her eyes followed him across the room.
> His hand reached for the gun.
> His feet led him to the car.
> Her finger pointed accusingly at him.

I'm sure everyone has read, if not written, variations of these sentences at one time or another. It's the language of genre fiction, in particular. In romance novels, eyes are always wandering; in crime fiction, hands are always reaching for something. Here are the problems with these sentences:

They're overused—hence, *default language*. Anyone could have written these sentences, and many already have.

They remind the reader of certain genres. If you write "His hand reached for the gun" and you're *not* writing a straight genre novel, your prose is going to read like parody.

These sentences are essentially inaccurate. The *hand* isn't reaching for the gun. A *person* is reaching for the gun. By writing sentences that are ever-so-slightly inaccurate, you're ever-so-slightly distancing the reader from the moment.

Oftentimes, these sentences are unintentionally funny, as when a student of mine wrote, "Her eyes bounced from the boy to the fountain to the girl and then back to the boy." Were these eyes superballs? Were they really bouncing? Intellectually, I know what the writer is trying to convey, but it's not good enough for the writer to plug in generic language while asking the reader to do the work of interpreting.

Redundancies

The first professional editor with whom I worked sent back one of my manuscripts with several words crossed out, all of them unnecessary because the subject and the action verb already implied the superfluous words. Interestingly, most of the words were body parts associated with physical gestures.

He shrugged his shoulders.
He blinked his eyes.
He nodded his head.

Notice how "his shoulders," "his eyes," and "his head" are implicit and unnecessary. What else could he possibly have shrugged, blinked, or nodded? And yet I run across these redundancies all the time, not only in my students' work but in published books. A good copyeditor should catch them, but often they slip by.

Here is my personal favorite, written by someone who wants to make damn sure that the reader understands what the gesture implies:

He nodded his head up and down in an affirmative manner and said, "Yes."

Bear in mind, the days of getting paid by the word for fiction are all but gone. Don't use fourteen words when two will do the job.

Not Cutting to the Sensory Detail Fast Enough

Imagine standing on the edge of the Grand Canyon and appreciating the view.

Now, imagine looking at it through cellophane. You may see some shapes here and there, but you will definitely miss the splendor of it.

Now, imagine looking at it through wax paper. Can you see anything? Are any of the images registering for what they really are?

Words can be the pane of glass through which the reader views the story's world, or they can function as cellophane or, worse, wax paper, obscuring what should be clear. Consider these sentences:

She looked at the car parked on the street.
She heard the sound of a window breaking.

In most contemporary fiction, the story's details are filtered through the point-of-view narrator. The fact that the narrator is experiencing these details through her senses is already implied by virtue of the story being told via that specific point of view. In other words, if a car is described in a story, I know that the narrator is seeing that car. I don't need to be told that the narrator is looking at that car. If a narrator hears something, I know that the narrator is hearing the sound being described without being told that the narrator is the one hearing it. The same holds true for any sensory detail in a story that's being filtered through a single narrator.

My advice is to cut more directly to the image or sound, or to whichever one of the five senses is being employed.

A car was parked on the street.
A window shattered nearby.

There are exceptions to every rule, and there are times when the writer will want to draw particular attention to the narrator observing, hearing, tasting, etc. When it's a problem, though, is when it's unnecessary. By writing "she saw" or "she heard," the writer is putting cellophane in front of the image. In the two revised sentences, the ratio of reader-to-experience is much closer to one-to-one than in the original sentences because unnecessary words have been trimmed away. In turn, the experience for the reader is more immediate and more visceral, pulling her more deeply into the story's world.

Favoring Adjectives and Adverbs
Instead of Precise Nouns and Verbs

At some point in the budding writer's career, probably as early as grade school, he is told to be descriptive. And what's the best way to be descriptive? Why, to use adjectives and adverbs, of course!

I don't have problems with the occasional use of an adjective or adverb. For instance, there really aren't many options for saying that a house is yellow except to write that it is a *yellow* house. I don't even have a problem with a *squat* house. Or even a *squat, yellow* house, for that matter. The problem is when it's a *beautiful* house. Or, worse, an *awesome* house. Where *squat* and *yellow* are specific and visual, *beautiful* and *awesome* are vague and abstract. All too often, beginning writers lean toward the vague and abstract instead of the specific and visual. And this is the chief problem with adjectives: they breed generic language.

A well-chosen adverb can do wonders for a sentence. Richard Yates was a master of the adverb, as in this excerpt from his brilliant novel, *Revolutionary Road*:

> . . . he pulled a stepladder raspingly from the wings . . .

Raspingly is perfect. It's succinct. It's unique. Even though it anthropomorphizes the ladder, which is sometimes a problem, it accurately captures the sound a ladder being dragged across a hard surface. And since the adverb is attempting to capture a *sound* rather than an *image*, the adverb isn't functioning as a lazy shortcut, which is all too often how adverbs are used.

Yates rises above the lot even when he uses adverbs visually. A few pages later in the novel, the play's director blinks *myopically*. Here, Yates takes a word (*myopic*) that's not usually turned into an adverb (*myopically*) and uses it in a way that's not forced or clunky. By this point, we already have a pretty good picture of the director in mind, so we don't need another visual attached to him. What's the function of using the word *myopically* if it's not to add a visual? Well, it *is* visual, but it also characterizes because it subtly works as a metaphor as well. All along, the director has been myopic, not just literally (although he does have bad eyesight) but in terms of how he views the people around him. By the time we read this sentence, the horror of the scene has already been shown to us, and to the director, who can't deny what a monumental failure his play has been, so it's especially poignant and devastating to see him blinking myopically at this point. In order for *myopically* to work in the sentence, however, it must work on a literal level first before it works as a metaphor, and it most assuredly does since the man wears glasses.

When adverbs don't work—and more often than not they don't—it's because the writer isn't fully imagining a scene and uses the adverb as an easy fix for a sentence. The adverb becomes default language, a generic word to plug in without the writer having to do the hard work of slowing down the moment and visualizing accurately what the scene looks like. That's why we see people talking *joyfully* or dancing *happily* or moving *grumpily* about the house. These are generic superimpositions over an action, and the reader is supposed to interpret what joyfully, happily, or grumpily look like. The problem is that what *I* think happily looks like isn't what *you* think it does. If a thousand people read one of my stories, I want a thousand people to walk away with the same images in their heads. They may have different shades of interpretation, given that each person brings his or her own personal experiences to bear, but the things the author can control are the specifics, most notably the images. If a thousand people have a thousand different interpretations of the word *joyfully*, it's a sign that the author has gone weak on the most important aspect of the story that she can control.

Every creative writing textbook in the history of the world—or, at least, every creative writing textbook I've ever seen—addresses the issue of why precise nouns and verbs are better than adjectives and adverbs. Even Strunk and White weigh in on this subject in *The Elements of Style*: "Write with nouns and verbs, not adjectives and adverbs. The adjective hasn't been built that can pull a weak or inaccurate noun out of a tight space." Even so, beginning writers often take issue with this very basic idea. Their argument is, "But I just *love* it when a scene is described so that I can see it."

Who wouldn't? But here's what I suspect happens. When a reader walks away from a book with a series of vividly rendered scenes still in his head, he tends to *think* that those scenes were flush with adjectives and adverbs, even when they weren't.

On more than one occasion, after telling audiences of aspiring writers to avoid adjectives and adverbs, someone has shouted out, "But what about

Cold Mountain? I love that book, and it's very visual!" Why *Cold Mountain* has become the go-to example for descriptive language, I don't know, but let's look at the first paragraph of Charles Frazier's novel:

> At the first gesture of morning, flies began stirring. Inman's eyes and the long wound at his neck drew them, and the sound of their wings and the touch of their feet were soon more potent than a yardful of roosters in rousing a man to wake. So he came to yet one more day in the hospital ward. He flapped the flies away with his hands and looked across the foot of his bed to an open triple-hung window. Ordinarily he could see to the red road and the oak tree and the low brick wall. And beyond them to a sweep of fields and flat piney woods that stretched to the western horizon. The view was a long one for the flatlands, the hospital having been built on the only swell within eyeshot. But it was too early yet for a vista. The window might as well have been painted grey.

Yes, this passage is very descriptive, but there are no superfluous adjectives or adverbs. The adjectives are used for the purpose of specificity: *long* wound; *triple-hung* window; *red* road; etc. The most extravagant use of adjectives would be "flat piney woods," and to be honest, I could do without the word "flat," which conjures an unnecessarily confusing image instead of a clear one. But by and large, the strength of the language in this passage remains the nouns and verbs, as in the first two sentences, with its powerful image of flies being drawn to the wound on Inman's neck. The reason you see what's happening is a result of the clarity of Frazier's writing. Allow me to rewrite those two sentences, adding adjectives and adverbs:

> At the first gesture of gloomy morning, pesky flies began stirring anxiously. Inman's sore eyes and the long, jagged wound at his neck hungrily drew them, and the soft sound of their flapping wings and the gentle touch of their tiny feet were soon more potent than a yardful of angry roosters in annoyingly rousing a man to wake.

Notice how the adjectives and adverbs muddy the nouns and verbs, making it more difficult to wade through the prose and see what's actually happening. Furthermore, they don't add anything that we didn't already know through inference in the original version.

That's not to say that some published writers don't use adjectives and adverbs in excess, and it doesn't mean that some readers don't enjoy them. I like to think of adjective and adverbs as condiments. What do you put condiments on? Usually, you use them on mass-produced, not-especially-high-quality meat in order to give it more taste. And if you've grown up, as I did, eating McDonald's all the time, almost every day, you're likely to crave the condiments on a high-grade cut of meat, because that's what you're used to. But the more high-grade cuts of meat you eat, the more refined your palate becomes, and eventually you realize that the condiments are smothering tastes that in and of themselves are wonderful.

Simile and Metaphor Overload

Similes and metaphors are great poetic devices to use in fiction. However, a reader will likely ignore a great simile or metaphor if it's surrounded by a half-dozen mediocre or bad ones. Therefore, use them sparingly.

Some inexperienced writers feel the urge to include a simile or metaphor in every sentence. In these stories, nothing is what it is; it's always something else. At a certain point, the reader won't even know what's grounded in reality and what's not because the touchstones of reality (that is, prose that hasn't been embellished by a simile or a metaphor) are gone. The result is hallucinatory.

The purpose of similes and metaphors is to illuminate something (an idea, a moment, a thing) in a new light, giving that idea/moment/thing a new dimension and, in turn, providing the reader a fresh, interesting look at said idea/moment/thing. If a reader encounters your simile or metaphor and says, "What?" you're in trouble. Remember that the purpose is to illuminate, not mystify.

Consider the first sentence of Doran Larson's short story "Morphine":

Despite tests and retests—her mammogram dittoed across clinic
walls like some sick Warhol print—Sarah had not understood her
disease until she'd sketched the body it was quickly dismantling.

Granted, not every reader will get the simile "like some sick Warhol" print;
not everyone is familiar with Andy Warhol. But this simile works because
Sarah, the story's limited third person narrator, is an artist, so the simile
makes sense in the context of who she is. And if the reader has seen Warhol's prints, they'll get the image. (Warhol's famous *Marilyn Diptych* contained fifty images of Marilyn Monroe, based on the same photograph.)

In some instances, the simile or metaphor is used for comic purposes.
Denis Johnson uses simile to good effect in his story "Emergency," about a
hospital janitor and orderly both on drugs. Consider this scene that takes
place at the county fair:

A champion of the drug LSD, a very famous guru of the love generation, is being interviewed amid a TV crew off to the left of the
poultry cages. His eyeballs look like he bought them in a joke shop.
It doesn't occur to me, as I pity this extraterrestrial, that in my life
I've taken as much as he has.

Denis Johnson reinforces the story's tone with simile ("His eyeballs look
like he bought them in a joke shop") and metaphor (". . . I pity this extraterrestrial . . ."). The tone is deadpan and darkly comic. Notice, too, what
Johnson *doesn't* do. The similes and metaphors aren't so overbearing that
the reader loses touch with reality. A less experienced writer might have
overloaded the similes and metaphors so as to imitate the altered state of
mind of a narrator on LSD. (See chapter "The Imitative Fallacy" for why I
would consider such a strategy a blunder.)

To give you an idea just how bad it can get, I wrote this purposely bad
passage overloaded with forced similes and metaphors:

The sound outside my window was like a crew of workmen using
jackhammers. It had been a long night, as if I were living on a planet
where night had no end, and when I glimpsed myself in the mirror the

next morning, I looked like a man who'd been hit by a truck. I looked
like I'd been to hell and back. The bags under my eyes were like the
kinds of bags you'd get at a grocery store, the paper kind, full of gro-
ceries. They were drooping weights under my eyes. It was that bad.

Yes, it was!

I wish I could say that I've never seen such passages in beginning writers'
stories, but I would be lying.

Referring to Memory, Thoughts, Recollections

In most fiction, a narrator's past informs their present, and most writers, in
an attempt to convey that past, will insert a flashback or, if they're writing
novels, several dozen flashbacks.

Flashbacks can be problematic for any number of reasons, but one diffi-
culty is figuring out a way to transition back in time. The default language
for these transitions tends to be "I was thinking back to a time when . . . ,"
or "I remembered . . . ," or "He recollected a period in his life . . . ," and
so on.

Unfortunately, these are clunky transitions that call attention to themselves. One might as well buy advertising space on a billboard that an-
nounces, FLASHBACK COMING! Remember those scenes in *Gilligan's
Island* or *Wayne's World* when a character begins rubbing his chin and everything goes fuzzy, melting into a flashback? That's more or less the effect
you achieve in a short story or novel when you use words like "remember,"
"thought back to a time when," or "recollect." The well-read reader or editor thinks, *Uh-oh, here it comes!*

Even in passages that don't go into full-blown flashbacks, these empty
words (*empty* because they're abstract words having to do with thoughts)
pile up but don't contribute in any substantive way to the scene. By substantive, I mean that these words aren't visual, don't push the plot forward, and
don't develop characterization:

As I lean back in my recliner, thinking, I recall the day from my past
when I walked into the kitchen and saw my mother sitting at the

table with her closest friend, Emma, and I remember the look of terror in Emma's eyes, but what I remember most is my mother telling me to keep myself occupied for the next few hours and stay out of the kitchen.

My advice is to find less intrusive ways to indicate memory. The least intrusive way is to use the past perfect to indicate when you want to indicate a transition in time. You may even want to add a clause that indicates how far back in time the scene is moving.

> When Lucy was five, her parents had opened their own shoe store on Main Street.

When you want to move back into the present, you insert the word "now" into a sentence.

> Now, Lucy walked the length of Main Street, staring into the ghosts of long-closed stores.

Granted, there's nothing fancy about this transition, but it does the trick in the least immediacy-deadening way possible. Furthermore, you eliminate all those useless words, like "thinking," "remembering," and "recalling."

If you want to get fancy and still remain immediate, you could connect scenes from the present to the past using images, which is more of a poetic device. The best example of this, to my mind, is Stuart Dybek's short story "Pet Milk," in which the unnamed narrator begins thinking about the past while he's watching Pet milk swirl into his coffee. That swirling imagery becomes the catalyst for time transitions, whether it's swirling clouds that the narrator is staring at or the swirling crème de cacao in a drink called the King Alphonse. The reader becomes aware on a subconscious level that there's a time transition each time we encounter that swirling image. Dybek's touch is light, and the imagery is subtly woven into the fabric of the story. Best of all, the language is visual and, as such, immediate.

Using Authorial Language

In most fiction, the story is usually filtered through a point-of-view narrator, which means, in most contemporary fiction, the reader is privy to what the narrator is privy to, not to what the author is privy to. (Omniscience has all but disappeared in contemporary fiction. Most contemporary literary fiction is written in either first person or third person limited, which means that the criteria for how a story is told these days is quite a bit different from the criteria for how a story was told in, say, the nineteenth century.)

Of course, what I'm saying isn't *entirely* true. In third person, especially —even when the reader is "inside the narrator's head"—the author frequently creeps into the story to provide us with information that the narrator knows but isn't necessarily thinking about at that particular moment. This is the fiction writer's sleight of hand, trying to balance those two things (the narrator's thoughts *and* the author's agenda), but the trick for any fiction writer is to do this in such a way that the reader isn't thinking about the writer, unless, of course, you're an experimental or postmodernist writer, which, for our purposes, you're not. No, invisibility is the goal and, therefore, the trick.

However, every once in a while the reader may run across a sentence that gives her pause. The reader may not even realize at first *why* the sentence stands out, but it does. And it leaves a bad taste in the reader's mouth. Oftentimes, the reason is because the author has unabashedly stepped into the story and made himself visible, as in these two sentences:

Nothing could disturb my bluish green eyes from the game.
She ran her fingers through her long, auburn hair.

Both sentences defy point of view logic by blatantly shifting attention away from what the narrator would be thinking to what the author wants to convey about the narrator. If the narrator of the first sentence is so attentive to "the game," as the sentence suggests, that same narrator wouldn't be thinking about the color of his or her eyes. The second sentence is subtler but no less problematic. I could probably let the word "long" stay as one of those moments when the author inserts herself into the story for a split second, but auburn? No. The agenda of the author—to describe what the narrator looks like—is too obvious now, shifting attention away from the story's moment as well as from what the narrator would, in all likelihood, actually be thinking about. Unless the narrator is looking into a mirror and thinking of changing the color of her hair, "long" and "auburn" (or at least "auburn") need to go.

Clichés

Every so often, a student will ask why he can't use a cliché. "But everyone knows what the cliché means," he'll argue. True enough. Also, it's common to find clichés in popular writing, so what's the big deal?

An original or distinct worldview is what separates mediocre writing from great writing. Clichés are antithetical to literary fiction's attempt to create that original worldview. What do I mean by worldview? In short, I mean that the story you write is distinct enough that only you could have written it. Think of Mark Twain's *The Adventures of Huckleberry Finn* or J. D. Salinger's *The Catcher in the Rye* or Flannery O'Connor's short stories or Margaret Atwood's *The Handmaid's Tale*. Each of these has a worldview that's as distinct as its author's DNA. Flannery O'Connor's short stories could *only* have been created by Flannery O'Connor. *The Handmaid's Tale* could *only* have been written by Margaret Atwood.

On the other hand, a story or novel laden with clichés could have been written by anyone. The worldview, if it could even be called that, would not be unique. It would be generic, commonplace, familiar. When a reader comes across a cliché, she is being asked by the writer to plug in her own image or flesh out a character. Clichés are the worst kind of default writing, because the writer isn't even trying. We all know what they look like:

She grinned like a Cheshire cat.
When I told her she had won, she grinned from ear to ear.
His eyes twinkled.

Her cheeks were rosy.
He was tall, dark, and handsome.
A single tear rolled down her cheek.
The big day was finally here!
What she said snapped me back to reality.

It's sometimes difficult to spot a cliché in your own work unless someone more experienced points it out for you. In graduate school, I wrote a scene in which a character gives another character a knowing look. My thesis advisor, an accomplished writer, noted that "knowing look" was a cliché. I thought: Really? Turns out she was right. I have seen knowing looks all over the place since then, always in amateurs' writing. So, when someone with more experience than you notes a cliché in your work, do yourself a favor and rethink it.

Documenting the Day

How long should a scene be? Do I tell the story chronologically or in some other order? Do I use flashbacks? At what point should the story begin?

In the chapter "Subject Matter," I provided definitions for "story" and "plot" from the book *Writing Fiction*: "A *story* is a series of events recorded in their chronological order. A *plot* is a series of events deliberately arranged so as to reveal their dramatic, thematic, and emotional significance."

Now, consider this opening to a short story:

The alarm clock rang, and I began my day. With the sun beating through the curtains, I rolled out of bed, yawned and stretched, then hopped into the shower. Once out of the shower, I had to decide what to wear.

Only one sentence into the story, and I'm already feeling sleepy. Three sentences in, and I want to throw the story in my fireplace. The author isn't making any choices essential to plotting a story. The story begins at the beginning of the day because the author's day begins similarly. Are we going to have to wade through every damned thing the narrator does? Probably.

(And why are people always *hopping* in these stories? They *hop* into showers; they *hop* out of cars. Writers, please take note: you're not writing about kangaroos!)

When the story documents the narrator's day in this way, we can pretty much give up on the notion that its author gave any consideration to selection—what to put in and what to leave out—because here is a writer who is going to make you watch the narrator put on his left shoe and then the right shoe. Our only hope is that the house the narrator is sitting in blows up, putting all of us out of our miseries.

The Curse of Foreshadowing

In grade school and high school, we're taught to find examples of foreshadowing in stories, so when we begin writing, we think that foreshadowing is a good thing to plant in our stories. Obvious foreshadowing, however, is an antiquated technique. It's the equivalent of wearing a monocle and driving a Model T in the year 2012.

An opening sentence like, "When I woke up, I knew something bad was going to happen," is cheesy because we've seen variations on it for over a hundred and fifty years. The hook is too obvious. "Little did Jack know that this was going to be the worst day of his life" is even worse because the author intrudes on the story. If Jack didn't know it was going to be the worst day of his life, why would we be privy to this information?

Foreshadowing wasn't always a bad technique. Here's the first line of Edgar Allan Poe's "The Black Cat," published in 1843:

> For the most wild yet most homely narrative which I am about to pen, I neither expect nor solicit belief.

By today's standards, Poe's prose here would be considered purple, his narrative techniques shopworn, but notice how much better his use of foreshadowing was than the two examples cited above. For starters, he doesn't reveal that something terrible is going to happen. He's a bit more vague, luring the reader into the story by suggesting that he won't believe what he's about to be told. Furthermore, the narrator acknowledges that he's *writing* the narrative, which has a different effect on the reader than a story which exists for the sake of existing, as most contemporary stories do. It's as though, in Poe's story, we're reading a diary or a confession.

Tim O'Brien took Poe's foreshadowing technique to a new level in *The Things They Carried*, a collection of linked short stories in which Tim O'Brien uses the form of the memoir, going so far as to name one of the characters Tim O'Brien and dedicating the book to many of the fictional characters in the stories. When the individual stories were first published, it wasn't always clear what genre it was—autobiography or fiction—and, as a result, O'Brien was able to manipulate the reader even more successfully than if he had been writing something that was clearly fiction. His use of foreshadowing is especially effective in his story "On the Rainy River":

> This is one story I've never told before. Not to anyone. Not to my parents, not to my brother or sister, not even to my wife. To go into it, I've always thought, would only cause embarrassment for all of us, a sudden need to be elsewhere, which is the natural response to a confession. Even now, I'll admit, the story makes me squirm. For more than twenty years I've had to live with it, feeling the shame, trying to push it away, and so by this act of remembrance, by putting the facts down on paper, I'm hoping to relieve at least some of the pressure on my dreams. Still, it's a hard story to tell.

True, this is foreshadowing, but it's also a tease that draws us closer, making us want to hear what the narrator is going to share with us. Because the story is in the first person, it doesn't defy point of view logic. We readers are the narrator's confidante, a role we are happy to play: *Yes, tell us!*

So, yes, Poe used foreshadowing to good effect, and a century and a half later, Tim O'Brien is still using it to good effect, but whenever you overtly manipulate the reader, you need to be aware that it may fall flat. The hair on the backs of our necks no longer rises when a story begins, "It was a dark and stormy night." We yawn instead. We close the book. We turn on the TV.

Lack of Exposition

Exposition is, simply put, information—one character's relationship to another, the name of a city, the age of the narrator, etc. Interestingly, though, exposition shapes how we feel about a narrator. Consider how your opinion of Larry changes with each of the following three sentences, in which I've tweaked the exposition.

> Larry stole a loaf of bread.
> Larry, sixty-seven years old and homeless, stole a loaf of bread.
> Larry, nineteen years old and the beneficiary of a trust fund, stole a loaf of bread.

Most readers probably don't feel much one way or the other about the narrator in the first sentence because we don't know anything about Larry. The second sentence is likely to evoke feelings of sympathy whereas the third may cause the reader to feel outrage. (Of course, depending upon your views of the homeless or trust funds, you may have different sentiments.) The point is that your feelings are likely to shift depending upon the exposition that's provided. It should be noted that a reader's empathy toward a character is a complex calculus of her own personal experiences and emotional maturity (or lack thereof), the characters' actions, and the exposition provided about a character.

In his essay "The Writers' Workshop," Frank Conroy discusses the relationship between the writer and reader with the given text (story or novel). In the essay, there is an illustration of an arc: the writer is on one side, the reader on the other. Conroy's theory is that there is a zone somewhere in the middle of that arc where the writer and reader should meet.

> The author, then, must write in such a way as to allow the reader's energy into the work. If the text is unintelligible, it falls short of the zone and the reader is blocked. If the text is preemptive and bullying, it goes past the zone, smothers the incoming energy, and the reader is blocked. In either case the dance of two minds necessary to bring a living narrative into existence is precluded.

I've witnessed the same results in regard to exposition. When the author leaves out necessary exposition or simply provides too little, the reader is bound to cross over into the writer's territory to fill in the gaps. The writer isn't doing his job in this instance. The result is that a dozen readers will walk away with a dozen different images in mind. On the other hand, the writer who crosses over into the reader's territory, describing everything *ad nauseum* while providing every last bit of exposition about a character is likely to suffocate the reader, burying her under minutiae. Therefore, the best thing for the writer is to find some kind of middle ground.

Here's an opening sentence that's too vague:

In the town where I grew up, Mary and I would go to the store and steal candy bars.

Whenever I ask my students to tell me about the town or store in this sentence, they always say, "I'm seeing a small town and a country store," even though there's no evidence pointing the reader in that direction. What's happening is that the reader is doing the work for the writer. Why a small town and a country store, though? These are stock images of America that we've seen on TV over and over and over. The reader is merely plugging in that which is familiar.

In contrast, consider this opening sentence:

On the north side of Chicago, when I was seventeen and only a month away from graduating from Evanston High School, I would slip away to Wal-Mart for lunch with Mrs. Mary Garrett, my Calculus teacher, and steal Slim Fast candy bars.

Here, the author may have overloaded the reader with too much information, at least for a single sentence, but notice how, although we have the same basic story as the previous sentence, our opinions about the characters have likely changed. The specific details in the second passage are challenging our expectations in a way that the first passage simply wasn't. Also, we now ask the right sorts of questions — *Why is the narrator stealing candy bars with a Calculus teacher? Why Slim Fast candy bars?* — unlike the first sentence, which prompts the wrong sorts of questions: *What kind of town? What kind of store?* The questions we ask after reading the first example are the result of the author's vagueness, whereas the questions we ask after reading the second example are because of the moral ambiguity of the situation. Moral ambiguity is interesting. Vagueness isn't.

Not Beginning in a Specific Time and Place

The few times I've taken on the daunting task of being a preliminary judge for a book contest, for which I would read upwards of one hundred and twenty short story collections (each collection averaging two hundred pages), I started noticing repetitions of problems that I might not have noticed had someone simply handed an individual short story to me. One recurring problem is when the author delays situating the short story in a specific time and place. I don't mean that the story has to begin, "It was 5:02 P.M. in Oak Lawn, Illinois, on December twentieth." What I mean is that the story needs to take place in real time instead of a general time. Consider this opening:

When I was a kid, we used to like to go sledding.

Imagine this story continuing in this mode for several paragraphs, where time remains amorphous: *I used to do this . . . I used to do that.* "Used to" means that the narrator could have been three years old, or five years old, or ten years old, or possibly all of those ages.

Such passages also tend to summarize rather than dramatize. It would be like watching a very long recap of a TV show's previous season. Usually, such recaps last only a few minutes, but imagine one lasting thirty or forty minutes. *Come on!* we would think. *Let's get started already!*—that is, of course, if we haven't already turned off the TV.

Readers want to hook into the meat of the story, and the longer the author delays placing the story in *real time*, the longer the reader feels as though she's floating outside the story, waiting for the real story to begin. Summarized action always feels like a prelude to something bigger. When that bigger thing never appears, readers become irritated.

In the following story opening, we're provided a time and place, but more importantly, the author situates the reader in a specific moment instead of a general moment.

> In 1978, the morning after the famous blizzard, I snuck out of the house while my parents slept. I took the metal lid off our garbage can, trudged up to the top of the highest street in our neighborhood, and then slid back down, clutching the lid's handle and screaming the whole way.

By placing the reader in a specific moment, the blurry past comes into focus, and we see specific images, such as the garbage can lid, and because we can see specific images, we can begin to infer certain things about the narrator, such as the socioeconomics of his life or the kind of neighborhood he lives in. As simple as that, the character has a past life the reader can *deduce* rather than one the reader is *told* about in summary for pages and pages. Which brings us to our next topic . . .

Backstory

Backstory is exactly what it sounds like: the story *before* the main story. Backstory may appear in the form of a sentence of exposition or as an extended, dramatized flashback. When used judiciously, backstory works in the service of the main story. When not used judiciously, the backstory suffocates the main story, and the story's structure looks like an ouroboros, the snake that swallows its own tail.

Another problem is when the author adds backstory before the reader has had a chance to get her toes wet in the main story. Here, the story moves forward in time for only a sentence or two before cutting to an extended flashback. The result is that the reader never feels engaged in the present-time story.

Let's say you're the passenger in a car and the driver has told you that you're going to stop first at the gas station down at the corner, and that each subsequent stop will be more interesting than the previous stop—in short, the function of plot is that we should be more invested in a story the deeper into it we get. So, the driver accelerates, and the car jumps forward a couple of feet, but then the driver jerks the car in reverse and backs up a couple of miles, leaving you to wonder what the hell is going on. The car finally moves forward again, back to the starting point plus a couple of feet, only to back up five miles this time. Your hope of ever reaching your destination—of ever going on the journey you thought you were going on— begins to die, just as a story or novel that clumsily overuses flashbacks to fill in backstory frustrates the reader to the point where she loses all interest in what she's reading. Even in this short paragraph, the tension is drained away by a needless flashback:

> As soon as I arrived at work, Mary Behrendt told me that my boss, Mr. Vik, was waiting to see me. "Are you sure?" I asked, and she nodded. My palms were sweating. The back of my neck was moist. Years ago, I had experienced a similar feeling. I was in either the fifth or sixth grade. It had been a day not at all unlike today. Back then, I was a skinny kid, and every day was exciting! I would ride my bike for hours and hours. Funny, isn't it, how you lose track of time when you're a kid?

Many readers feel a flicker of disappointment when a flashback appears, which means that the author needs to make it interesting. Damn interesting.

When backstory is used to provide easy, unearned explanations for a character's behavior—for example, the narrator was beaten as a child; this is why he goes on a killing spree—the experienced reader loses patience. *Puh-leaze!* we think.

Occasionally, the backstory is legitimately the main story, but in vast majority of stories I read where backstory is overused, this isn't the case. The writer should have worked harder to engage the reader with the present-time story.

If backstory is really, truly necessary, the writer should make the reader crave it first before handing it over. That's not to say that you should withhold essential information from the reader. Essential information should be revealed early on, lest you risk looking like the cheap writer who plays sophomoric games with the reader. But if it's not essential, hold it back until the reader absolutely needs it. And guess what? You may discover that the reader doesn't need it, after all.

Cramming Too Much into the Container

The length of a short story or novel is its container. It's possible, I suppose, to write a short story that takes place over the entire length of the Civil War, but chances are that most attempts do this would result in stories that are mostly summarized, with vague language and broadly drawn characters, and a conflict that's more external (and probably more superficial) than internal.

There are ambitious short stories that successfully cover long periods of time, such as Harriet Doerr's "Edie: A Life," but these are rare. Doerr's story works, in part, because it's written in a series of dramatized vignettes. The effect is like staring at a painting by a pointillist: you see (and appreciate) the individual dots, but when you stand back, you see the larger image that all those dots comprised. Likewise, there are writers who take small moments and grow them into novels, as Nicholson Baker has done, most notably in his first two books, *The Mezzanine* (a novel about a one-story escalator ride) and *Room Temperature* (a novel about a father bottle-feeding his baby for twenty minutes). Like Doerr, Baker's choice of what to write about is very deliberate, and it's clear that both authors, Doerr and Baker, understood the potential perils of what they were undertaking and worked against those pitfalls.

Most novice writers try to cover way too much time or attempt to juggle way too many storylines in a few pages instead of isolating a smaller moment, a moment worthy of a good short story, or a series of very focused, smaller moments (as Doerr does in "Edie: A Life"), and then putting their energies into fully dramatizing those moments and exploring their potential. My students' ambitiousness, in regard to how much they think they can actually cover in a short story, usually gets the better of them. At some point, the writer needs to consider the container they're filling: is it too small, too large, or just right?

Another frequent problem is when a story needlessly sprawls over a long period of time. Whenever possible, crunch time. If you have an idea for a short story that takes place over many years, ask yourself if it will work over the course of a month or a week. If it takes place over a week, can it happen in a day? If it takes place over twenty-four hours, would it work having it take place over an hour? Crunching time is one of the most effective ways to make a piece of prose more immediate. One of the reasons for the popularity of the TV show *24*—and the classic movie *High Noon*, for that matter—was that it supposedly took place in real time; as a result, every moment was infused with more intensity, even moments that weren't particularly intense in and of themselves. The same is true in stories and novels. Crunching the time, if it's possible to crunch the time, gives more immediacy to each scene.

Gratuitous Details instead of Details Filtered through a Distinct Consciousness

As I've already mentioned, I judge contests. During one particular fourteen month period, I looked at over two hundred short story collections alone.

I can tell you that half were easily pushed aside because the stories were written by people who didn't appear to have read a short story written in the past hundred years, or because the stories were barely literate, or because they were thinly-veiled autobiographical anecdotes of the worst kind. I know this sounds like a cruel assessment, but it's true. These were, by and large, unpublishable manuscripts.

Now, the other half of those manuscripts (with the exception of about five of them) fall into a category that I want to spend some time on here. These manuscripts were competent, even well-written, but they lacked something vital. They lacked *life*. It's the difference between a life-like mannequin and a real person. No matter how life-like the mannequin may seem, it still doesn't breathe.

The question, then, is how does one breathe life into a story? For me, the difference is whether or not the author has submerged herself into the consciousness of the point-of-view narrator in such a way that everything—

especially the details—is filtered through that particular and unique perspective. When the author *isn't* doing this, the prose is workmanlike, the exposition is often overt rather than implied, and the entire story reads like words on a page instead of being what it should be: a visceral experience for the reader.

The vast majority of competent but lifeless stories contained passages like this one:

> Jack walked into the room. The room was furnished with a floral-print sofa, an antique roll-top desk, and a rocking chair. Several paintings adorned the walls: portraits, mostly. Jack stepped onto the Oriental rug and hung his coat on an oak rack.

The details here are list-like. The room is decorated with *this* and *this* and *this* and *this*. The details are also superfluous. Who cares if the coat rack is oak? Does the fact that the rack is oak change what we know about Jack? Can you *see* the coat rack better knowing that it's oak as opposed to, say, hickory? I doubt it.

The primary fault with this passage—and with the numerous manuscripts I saw in the book contest—is that the author is writing about Jack instead of inhabiting Jack's consciousness. The passage feels written, not lived. For the reader, the result is that we intellectually process what's happening in the story, but we don't *feel* it. Also, nothing about Jack is inferred in this passage. Jack is nothing more than a fictional construct moving through an authorially decorated room.

Now, notice what happens when those same details are filtered through Jack's consciousness:

> Jack felt as though he'd stepped into a museum. He was afraid to touch anything—the pristine roll-top desk, the spindly coat rack— and he certainly didn't want to sit down on furniture that was bound to disintegrate beneath him. Every person inside every portrait on the wall seemed to be looking down at him, watching his every move, and when he averted his eyes, he realized that he'd tracked mud onto

an Oriental rug that was probably worth more than he'd made all of last year.

Ah ha! Details are no longer simply details. Details are vehicles through which Jack negotiates his life. And what we learn about Jack is *inferred* through the way Jack interprets those things he sees. The fact that he's afraid to touch anything suggests that he feels out of his element. The fact that every portrait seems to be looking at him suggests some paranoia. We can also intuit something about his socioeconomic lot through his observation about the Oriental rug being "probably worth more than he'd made all of last year." In only a few short sentences, we know so much more about Jack than we knew about him after reading the first example. Most importantly, what we know about him is inferred. There is no authorial voice overtly telling us that Jack is feeling out of place, slightly paranoid, and of lesser means than the person he's visiting. What's more is that we feel legitimate tension in those few sentences, and it's this tension that fuels narrative momentum, causing us to read on.

Remember how I said half of the book-length manuscripts were unpublishable and the other half, with the exception of five, were competent but lifeless? Those five that I had set aside were the ones I couldn't stop reading. Those were the ones that came fully alive while the others remained inert. As soon as I began reading the first of these five manuscripts, I pushed all the competent ones aside, which, until then, I had been futilely trying to rank.

Using Weak Sentence Structures

It's been said that syntax—sentence structure—is prose's music. If you read *One Hundred Years of Solitude* or the short fiction of Eudora Welty, you'll certainly hear that music. John Updike is another writer whose sentences approximate music. Read aloud the first paragraph from his short story "The Lovely Troubled Daughters of Our Old Crowd":

Why don't they get married? You see them around town, getting older, little spinsters already, pedaling bicycles to their local jobs or walking up the hill by the rocks with books in their arms. Annie Langhorne, Betsey Clay, Demaris Wilcombe, Mary Jo Addison: we've known them all since they were two or three, and now they've reached their mid-twenties, back from college, back from Year Abroad, grown women but not going anywhere, not New York or San Francisco or even Boston, just hanging around here in this little town letting the seasons wash over them, walking the same streets where they grew up, hanging in the shadows of their safe old homes.

Notice how there's a progression to the lengths of the sentences: five words, twenty-nine words, seventy-eight words. Notice, too, how the repetitions, lists, and patterns of words and clauses within the last sentence provide a backbeat to the content: the list of names (*Annie Langhorne, Betsey Clay, Demaris Wilcombe, Mary Jo Addison*); the list of ages of the women when the narrator first met them (*two or three*) and their ages now (*mid-twenties*); repetition of "back from" (*back from college, back from Year Abroad*); list of city names (*not New York, not San Francisco or even Boston*); the three dependent clauses, back-to-back, spiraling like a toy top to end the sentence (*letting the seasons wash over them, walking the same streets. . . , hanging in the shadows. . .*).

Not every writer has to use such complex syntax. Hemingway didn't. Flannery O'Connor didn't. Raymond Carver didn't. And yet their prose is still aesthetically pleasing, closer to the stripped-down music of Philip Glass than Charlie Parker, but musical nonetheless.

A writer may have a tin ear, incapable of hearing the flatness of his sentences. Occasionally, I'll read a short story by an aspiring writer that sounds like a flat-voiced robot speaking to me: *I ate cereal for breakfast. I washed my car. I drove to my friend's house. I knocked on her door.*

The problem often has less to do with a writer's ear than with the writer's limited repertoire. Beginning writers tend to use only a handful of sentence structures, and two of those structures are particularly weak, especially in terms of immediacy. The first weak sentence structure includes a dependent clause that begins with "as" followed by a noun or pronoun.

It doesn't make a difference if the dependent clause precedes or follows the independent clause; it's weak.

As she opened the door, she began pointing at her sister.

The first problem with this syntax is that, as stated above, it's overused. The second problem is that it suggests simultaneous action: she's opening the door *at the same time that* she's pointing at her sister. Is this really what the author wants us to visualize? Is this how the scene would really play out in real life? Writers who overuse this syntax often don't visualize what they're actually writing. Oftentimes, the two clauses are meant to be concurrent actions, not simultaneous, as in the following sentence:

He wiggled out of his coat, as he reached for the telephone.

The action here is inaccurate and, as such, preposterous. Here's what the author really wants us to visualize:

He wiggled out of his coat then reached for the telephone.

The "as he"/"as she"/"as they"/"as it" works best when the subjects aren't the same. For instance:

She told me she was leaving as I chewed my gum and stared at her.

Whenever the reader is required to visual two simultaneous actions, the immediacy of the moment is going to be somewhat diminished for the simple reason that the reader is being asked to visualize something slightly more complicated. This is a negligible point if the reader is sparingly asked to do this, and it's no big deal when the actions are indeed meant to be seen as simultaneous actions. When the author uses this syntax in a way that inaccurately portrays the actions, you can bet that the immediacy will be all but killed.

Here's an example of the other weak and overused syntax:

Walking into the room, he pushed open the door and saw what they were doing.

This syntax opens with a participial phrase, and it presents the same problems as the other weak syntax above in that it suggests simultaneous action even when the action, as in this example, probably isn't really simultaneous. As with the other syntax, authors who use this one don't know when to stop. In fact, authors tend to use one or the other, and when I suggest that they vary syntax, they tend to simply switch it to the other one, solving nothing.

This syntax presents even more problems than the other problematic syntax. Notice how the reader is presented with an action before the character who's doing that action is introduced. The reader can't picture who's doing what until she reaches the subject that follows the comma. This is deadly for immediacy. This may not be a huge problem for a sentence like this one: "Laughing, he shook his head." But the longer the dependent clause, the less immediacy the prose will have, as in this sentence:

Listening in on all the various things they were saying about Uncle Joe and Aunt Thelma, Jimmy reached down and touched his toes.

In this sentence, it takes *sixteen* words before we reach Jimmy, the person who's listening. This may not seem like a big deal, but when the majority of sentences in a story are written using this syntax, the words fail to transform into an experience for the reader, and the sentences become nothing more than a string of words for the reader to plod through.

Another problem with this syntax is that it lends itself to dangling modifiers. A dangling modifier in this instance is when the opening verb has no connection to the subject:

Staring out the window, the city spread out before him.

This sentence is telling the reader that the city is staring out the window, which, of course, isn't what the author means. The author simply didn't catch the dangling modifier. In stories where the author is hooked on this syntax, I usually see at least one dangling modifier.

During the course of a semester, someone will inevitably ask me, "So, how else would you write it?" as though there are only three ways to structure a sentence. What the beginning writer really needs to do is expand his repertoire. In *The Art of Fiction*, John Gardner suggests typing out a story like James Joyce's "The Dead." I would suggest something a little less dramatic and more contemporary. Back when I edited my first few anthologies, I would have to type some of the previously published stories so that there would be a file for them, and among the authors whose stories I typed were Richard Russo, Margaret Atwood, Bharati Mukherjee, and Stephen King—writers with vastly different prose styles. The experience of sitting down and actually typing words they had written was unlike any analysis of prose styles I had ever done because it put me inside their heads and forced me to write sentences in ways that would never have occurred to me. It's one thing to look at a sentence and think about it; it's another thing altogether to type it. The act of typing, which is physical as well as mental, helped to imprint a variety of sentence structures in my brain in a way that simply looking at them wouldn't have accomplished. It's the difference between reading about driving a car and actually driving one. If you've never driven a car before, reading about one may give you a sense of what it's like to drive one, but it doesn't in any way compare to actually driving it, where you'll encounter a dozen different nuances each minute.

No Control of Psychic Distance

Psychic distance is the distance that the reader feels from the narrator. The reader may feel far away, as in, "It was 1888. A blue house sat in the middle of a snow-covered field," or she may feel inside the character's head, as in, "*All those stupid people*, she thought, *they never left her alone . . . stupid, stupid, stupid*," or she may feel somewhere in between, as in, "Mary stepped out of her house and looked up at the sky. It was what her mother would have called a *dreary day*, with its grey clouds and touch of cold in the air, but Mary preferred these sorts of days."

I've already covered psychic distance in the chapter "Beginnings," so I won't go into great length here except to say that controlling psychic distance is the primary goal for maintaining immediacy. In the "Common Errors" section of *The Art of Fiction*, John Gardner writes, "A piece of fiction containing sudden and inexplicable shifts in psychic distance looks amateur and tends to drive the reader away."

One level of remove isn't necessarily better than another. As I noted earlier, Ernest Hemingway tended to write from a great distance, rarely dipping into internal thought, let alone internal monologue. William Faulkner, on the other hand, tended to remain very internal. Now, imagine a story where one sentence reads as though it came from a Faulkner story while the next sentence reads as though it came from a Hemingway story, and where the sentences randomly continue to go back and forth between these polar extremes of psychic distance. It would be jarring to say the least, probably even headache-inducing. And yet it happens all the time.

You're the writer; you should be in control. The more in control you are, the more easily the reader will sink into the pages she's reading.

A Fixation on Physical Description

Beware of writing physical descriptions that read like a police-issued all-points bulletin:

> Six-foot-two, of medium build, and with piercing blue eyes, Jack walked up to me and said hello.

Characterization comes alive because of what a character says and does, not necessarily because of what the character looks like. Better to find something that will individualize the character. Oddly enough, the APB description above, though ultra-specific, actually creates a generic character. Is it *important* that he's six-foot-two or that his eyes are blue? And why are we privy to those details at that particular moment? If he wants to run a marathon but weighs four hundred pounds, then his weight would be an important detail. Otherwise, who cares?

This isn't to say that you can't write a descriptive paragraph about one of your characters. Here's a paragraph from Benjamin Percy's story "Refresh, Refresh" that works wonderfully as a passage that both characterizes and describes:

My father wore steel-toed boots, Carhartt jeans, a T-shirt advertising some place he had traveled, maybe Yellowstone or Seattle. He looked like someone you might see shopping for motor oil at Bi-Mart. To hide his receding hairline he wore a John Deere cap that laid a shadow across his face. His brown eyes blinked above a considerable nose underlined by a gray mustache. Like me, my father was short and squat, a bulldog. His belly was a swollen bag and his shoulders were broad, good for carrying me during parades, and at fairs, when I was younger.

Percy continues describing the father but not in terms of what he looks like. Rather, he zeroes in on things the father likes and the things he does. But notice that when Percy *is* physically describing the father the descriptions are either very specific ("a T-shirt advertising some place he had traveled, maybe Yellowstone or Seattle) or comparative ("Like me, my father was short and squat, a bulldog."). The "Yellowstone or Seattle" T-shirt detail suggests a life for this character beyond the confines of the story, which is precisely what a writer should strive to achieve so that the reader believes in the character's existence. By paragraph's end, I have a good sense of the father, whereas if Percy had written, "Five-foot-two, 225 pounds, brown hair and brown eyes, my father walked into the store," I'd have skimmed over the lazy details. If I want to read such bland descriptions, I'll go to the post office and read "Wanted" posters.

Searching for Substitute Words
Instead of Using Commonplace Ones

I rarely see this problem, but the fact that I have seen it more than once suggests that it's deserving of a warning. This problem is when the author thinks it's "poetic" to find new ways to describe an object rather than simply calling the object what it is. When the author does this repeatedly throughout an entire story, the reader begins to feel as though she's dropped down into the rabbit hole where the Mad Hatter has been awaiting her arrival. In other words, it's excruciatingly surreal.

Frank rode his bicycle all over town. His two-wheeled vehicle was made for a girl, and he feared, as he pedaled through the municipality, that someone would point and laugh at him. He pumped the spikey devices harder, picking up speed through the settlement.

Two-wheeled vehicle? Municipality? Spikey devices? Settlement?

Granted, you want to avoid repetition when you write, but do you want to sacrifice clarity? And do you really want the reader to laugh at you, because that's what's going to happen here.

Many years ago, when I pointed out this problem in a workshop, the story's author leaned toward a classmate and, cutting her eyes toward me, said, "I guess *some* people don't like poetic language!"

Fair enough. And when some people go to restaurants, they like to order a ribeye steak, not a slice of cooked meat from a grass-grazing quadruped often seen at the side of flattened, gray, pebbly material upon which people drive their four-wheeled, motorized contraptions.

EXERCISES

1. Time to get it out of your system. Write a story (no longer than ten pages) in which you commit every single one of these errors. Go for it!

2. Take a story you've worked hard on and circle every problem with immediacy you find in it. It's unlikely that you would commit every problem above—fingers crossed—but which ones did you commit the most? It's good to know what your tics are so you can look for them after first drafts or, ideally, before you commit them.

3. Choose four authors with starkly different prose styles. For instance, you could choose Toni Morrison (dense prose), Raymond Carver (spare prose), Eudora Welty (colloquial prose), and Elmore Leonard (accessible prose). Now, type at least two complete pages from one of their stories or novels. Type it accurately, indenting

where it needs to be indented, punctuating correctly, etc. Now, type up your observations about the experience. Were you exposed to new sentence structures? Does the experience make you want to emulate any of these writers? What was it like to be inside each author's head, if only to transcribe their prose?

Pop Culture

I'M A HYPOCRITE. I warn my students against using pop culture references in their fiction, citing for them stories from the early twentieth century that are unreadable now because we don't recognize the pop culture references in them. Even recent stories will include meaningful winks at one-hit wonders that have already vanished from our memories. Culturally speaking, we have short attention spans, and if in fifteen years your story needs footnotes—hell, let's say five years—you may have a problem. Worse, if you can't recognize pop culture references in your own story a few years after you've written it, you're really in trouble. The issue, I tell my students, isn't writing for posterity, which is out of your hands. The issue is accessibility, which is something you can control.

But, as I say, I'm a hypocrite. My own work is flush with pop culture references. In my novels and stories, you'll find Peter Frampton, KISS, Styx, Journey, Cheap Trick, *Planet of the Apes*, *The Chinese Connection*, *Beneath the Planet of the Apes*, *Buster and Billie*, *Escape from the Planet of the Apes*, *Walking Tall*, *Conquest of the Planet of the Apes*, *Enter the Dragon*, *Battle for the Planet of the Apes*, Evel Knievel, Yes's "Roundabout," The Doors's "Light My Fire," Led Zeppelin's "Moby Dick," Farrah Fawcett-Majors, W. C. Fields, Olivia Newton-John, the *Gong Show*, and even Edgar Bergen's ventriloquist doll, Mortimer Snerd.

Whenever I decide to use a pop culture reference in my own fiction, though, I ask myself three questions:

1. Does it make sense in the context of the moment, or is it simply there for the sake of being there? In other words, is it an organic part of the scene, or is it doing nothing more than evoking a time

period? For me, when a pop culture reference works best, it needs to be a part of the larger fabric of the scene. That's not to say that I'm not guilty of trying to evoke a specific time period with a reference, but I try to avoid it, and if I catch myself putting in a detail simply for wallpaper, I'll take it out.

2. Where is the reference coming from—the consciousness of the character or the author? I'm always writing in the margins of my students' stories "authorial, authorial, authorial," by which I mean that the reference is coming from the author and not, as it should be, the narrator's consciousness. It's too easy to be authorial, just as it's always easier to stand above something and look down on it. It's much harder to submerge yourself into the consciousness of a point-of-view character and ask yourself, over and over, these questions: Is this something the character would actually think? Is this faithful to who this character is, to the very particular and idiosyncratic galaxy of stuff (for lack of a better word) that comprises this character's life, or am I just being clever here? It's really a question of accuracy. It's what John Gardner might have called "intellectual honesty."

3. Finally, there's tone to consider. You're unlikely to find Cormac McCarthy referencing the *Planet of the Apes* franchise. Why? Because such a reference would throw the tone of his books out of whack. Imagine, if you will, a reference to the watermelon-smashing comedian Gallagher in the latest Doris Lessing novel. And yet, such a reference wouldn't necessarily be out of place in a short story by Lorrie Moore. Tone is almost always interlocked with the writer's vision—that elusive thing we call worldview that often defines for us a writer's entire body of work—and since my younger students haven't yet discovered what their worldview is (or haven't yet mastered controlling it), I will not infrequently find pop culture references sneaking in at the wrong moments, derailing scenes that were tonally heading one way until the appearance of a jarring pop culture reference left readers scratching their heads.

These three questions are all related to the artistic aspect of writing, but there is also another one that may be the most important question of all: is my work inviting readers inside, or am I excluding large segments of readers? This isn't an issue of mass appeal as much as it is an issue of mass exodus. It's not very difficult to shoo readers away. It's much more challenging to lure them closer, even harder to keep them close.

EXERCISES

1. Pick a book by a writer known for using pop culture references (for example, Bret Easton Ellis) and analyze a few pages of it. Do the pop culture references meet the criteria above? If not, does it still work?

2. Pick an enduring pop culture reference from your youth and figure out a way to write a very short story (no longer than five pages) around it. Make sure that the references meet the criteria above.

3. What might be some forgotten pop culture references from your youth, the kinds of references that most people would have forgotten or that a younger generation wouldn't know at all? Choose one and write a very short story (five to eight pages) in which this obscure reference is the centerpiece. Be sure to follow the criteria above.

Humor

I'LL ADMIT IT: my tastes are low-brow. I'm an academic only because I happen to teach at a university.

At an on-campus interview several years ago, I was asked about the humor that runs through my fiction and who my influences were. While I stared blankly ahead, a few of the professors interviewing me offered up a plethora of literary examples. I suppose I could have agreed with them, and then we all could have moved ahead without the awkward silence. But I didn't. If I'd had any chance at the job, I blew it right there. The thing is, no one they mentioned *had* been an influence. It was, however, a question worth thinking about, even if it meant standing there and looking like an idiot. To my detriment, I'd rather look like an idiot than say something I don't really believe. Hence, years of unemployment.

I hadn't ever given any serious thought to my humor influences before that interview, but the answer—the truth—is that I read virtually nothing the first eighteen years of my life. Instead, I watched (and listened to) endless comedy, in one form or another. I bought 8mm movies of Charlie Chaplin and Laurel and Hardy. Every Saturday at 2:30, I watched Abbott and Costello. I watched the Marx Brothers whenever they were on, or the Three Stooges, or even second-rate comedy teams, like the Ritz Brothers. I bought albums with vaudeville routines on them, typed up the routines, and memorized them. I practiced them in front of my dog. I listened to cassettes of old radio shows with Jack Benny and Edgar Bergen. In the seventh grade, I started writing a book about old-time comedians. I finished it at the end of eighth grade—two hundred pages of prose typed on a cast-iron Royal typewriter. Girls scribbled in my autograph book, "Remember me when you're famous!" *Oh yes*, I thought, *I will*. I wrote to every publisher

in New York; no one wanted to see it. But it wasn't just the old-time comedians that interested me. I listened to Cheech and Chong, to George
Carlin, to Bill Cosby, to Richard Pryor. I started watching *Saturday Night
Live* beginning with their second show. I saw Steve Martin in concert
back when he could pack the largest amphitheater in Chicago. He wore an
arrow through his head and sang "King Tut." I stole his routine and won
second place in my eighth-grade talent contest. Disco dancers won first. I
savored everything that was funny or supposed to be funny. I bought a lot
of books—the *idea* of books interested me, especially since I had written
one—but I read next to nothing, unless it was a book about comedians.

How could I not have internalized all of this comedy? How could I
not have picked up a thing or two about the ways in which humor works?
Many years later, and only after writing several short stories featuring a narrator named Hank—a good kid in eighth grade—and his troublemaking
friend Ralph, who had failed both third and fifth grades, did I realize that
they were a comedy team, a straight man and a comic, and the rhythms of
their dialogue resembled the rhythms of a vaudeville team. Even the dy-
namic of their relationship—a con artist and a naïf—looked an awful lot
like the template for, say, Abbott and Costello. And so it is my contention
that there's much to be learned in the so-called low art.

But it's also my contention that one's sense of humor is innate, and that
while you may be able to teach the mechanics of comic writing, you can't
conjure up the soul of a comic out of thin air. It's either in the DNA or
it isn't.

A few semesters ago, I showed a *Saturday Night Live* clip to my fiction
writing class, the point of which is now lost on me. Perhaps I had nothing
prepared for the day; I don't remember. Anyway, I showed the clip, and
everyone laughed, but one young woman laughed nervously, and when we
began discussing the clip, she admitted that she didn't see what was funny
about it. Before anyone could say anything, she added that she didn't understand *any* of the humor on *Saturday Night Live*. This wasn't a comment
on the show's declining quality or the fact that Lorne Michaels no longer
seems to know when to end a skit; no, she was admitting that all humor of

this variety escaped her. *All of it.* This, I should note, was a student with a 4.0. She wasn't dumb. But over the two semesters that she took classes with me, I saw time and again the fear in her eyes when classmates started to laugh at one thing or another, and then she would join in uncertainly, only to say, "What? . . . *What?*"

Furthermore, I tend to believe (and, I should note, I have no proof for anything I say: I'm an English professor, after all) that the comic sensibility you are born with is the same one you'll have for the rest of your life. That's not to say that it won't become more sophisticated or more complex. It will. And it's not to say that you won't be able to appreciate other types of humor. You will. But the *sorts* of humor that most appeal to you at two and three years old will appeal to you at forty-three. As much as I admire Dorothy Parker, I would still rather watch Moe poke Curly in the eyes than read Ms. Parker's work. In fact, I never tire of watching Moe poke Curly in the eyes. Consider Moe, if you will, that ball of fury, that tightly-wound epitome of pure rage. We may not want to admit it, but Moe is us, really. He's us every time we talk to a stupid boss; he's us every time one of our colleagues does something that makes us look bad; he's us every time someone cuts us off when we're driving. The difference is this. We do nothing. At most, we flip someone the bird when the person isn't looking. But Moe: he does what all of us wish to do. He pokes his cohorts in the eyes. He hits them with a sledgehammer. He picks up a cheese grater and gives them a good scrape across the face. Everything within his reach is a weapon: a flowerpot, a band saw, a vise grip. He's us without restraint. Imagine a world in which we could clonk our boss over the head without consequence. I loved Moe when I was three, but in the intervening years the weight of Moe has accumulated, and I love him anew for the larger things Moe represents, the metaphor of Moe, and for that, he's funnier than he's ever been.

But I digress.

Let me say this: there's nothing funnier than watching someone fall into a manhole. I learned the hard way. Drunk one night and walking across a lawn at a party, I failed to notice the drainage ditch. One minute, my friends were watching me walk toward them; the next, I simply wasn't there. I was stuck—wedged, actually—between two concrete slabs. What does this tell me about the humorous scenario? That it's about point of view. It's about perspective. But it's also about the absurd, to some extent. It's about the unexpected coming to fruition.

Take this story. A hundred percent true. For me, it embodies all that one ever needs to know about the art of humor. Lincoln, Nebraska. Mid-1990s. Football Saturday. Bear in mind, these were the glory years when the Cornhuskers were a powerhouse football team with two national championships behind them, a third championship looming before them. You could hear it in the streets that season, that word that's not really a word: three-peat. It became a mantra, an incantation, a riddle, like something spoken by the witches in *Macbeth*. *Can last year's repeat become this year's three-peat?* My then-girlfriend, Amy, and I had decided to go downtown for pizza and a beer. Our friend—let's call him Ned—came along. It was bone-chillingly cold that day, and we had to park several blocks from the restaurant. Furthermore, the Huskers had lost their game, a rarity in those days, and so the mood of the town was palpably somber. On our way to the bar, we passed three portable outdoor toilets, sometimes called Johnny-on-the-Spots, sometimes Porta-Johns. Our friend, like some kind of wild animal, preferring to do his business outside than inside, had to stop. He chose the middle one. Afterward, we continued on, enjoyed our pizza and beer, and then headed back to the car.

"I need to stop again," Ned said.

"We were just in the bar," Amy said. "Why didn't you go there?"

"I'd rather go here," he said, and, again, he stepped inside the middle Porta-John.

To escape the ear-numbing wind, Amy and I stood behind an eye-level billboard that ran along the sidewalk. In the distance, I saw a lonely figure, a young man wearing a cowboy hat and a large belt buckle but no coat. His shirt had pearl buttons and his jeans looked ironed. No doubt he had driven here all the way from western Nebraska for the game. It's important to note that I normally don't talk to strangers. In fact, I never initiate conversations with strangers. Strangers scare me. This may be because I'm a magnet for every crazy person in a room. I'm the one they'll gravitate toward, the one they want to confess to, so I avoid them. It's also important to note that I am not cheery by nature. (I'm not *not* cheery; I'm just not cheery.) But for some inexplicable reason, I couldn't resist on that particular cold Saturday: just before the young man from western Nebraska reached us, I stepped out from behind the billboard and cheerily asked, "Where's your coat?" to which he replied, "Huskers lost!" then pivoted on his heel and kicked the middle Porta-John as hard as he could. He kicked it with the flat of his boot and then continued walking. The Porta-John tilted to the point where we were sure it would fall over onto the street, but then it started to tilt back the other way. We could hear our friend inside screaming. The Porta-John tilted toward us for a moment before tilting back the other way. Finally, it righted itself, and out came our friend, yelling, "What the HELL?" Amy and I were on the ground, on our knees, bent over and laughing. We couldn't talk; we could barely breathe. I pointed down the street in the direction the cowboy had walked, but no one was there.

Why is this funny? Allow me to get academic here for a moment. As philosopher D. H. Monro points out, there are three theories to humor: the incongruity theory, the superiority theory, and the relief theory. The incongruity theory occurs when the outcome is radically different from the one we had expected. I say, "Where's your coat?" and the boy responds, "Huskers lost!" and tries to kick over the Porta-John with my friend inside. It's the incongruity between what's said and what's done that's funny. The superiority theory is when we laugh at someone else's blunder, foolishness, or (in this instance) bad luck. My friend who was in the Porta-John has never fully appreciated the humor of the situation, but everyone else has—and they have for one reason: we're not him. Furthermore, we're *glad* we're not him. The relief theory occurs when a comic moment—sometimes a funny comment—is inserted into a tension-filled moment. The tension in the story comes from whether the Porta-John is going to tip over or not, but the comic moment comes when it finally rights itself and my friend bursts out of it, yelling, "What the HELL?"

These are but three theories on humor and how it works. Study them. Memorize them. But I'm not sure it will matter at the end of the day. Humor is instinctual. You can't teach someone who's not funny how to be funny. If you still don't believe me, I've come up with a formula to *become* funny: "John McNally's Sure-Fire Formula for Becoming Funnier in Thirty Days!" If at the end of the month you have not laughed at anything you've watched or read, and if no one has laughed at anything you've written or done, then you're not funny. Sorry.

John McNally's Sure-Fire Formula for Becoming Funnier in Thirty Days!

* Day 1: Read Mark Twain. Any Mark Twain will do. Twain pretty much embodies every mode of nineteenth-century humor in America, which, in turn, pretty much set the stage for every form of humor that followed.

* Day 2: Spend the day watching Charlie Chaplin, Laurel and Hardy, Fatty Arbuckle, Buster Keaton, and Harold Lloyd comedies. Stick to their silent movies. There's much to be learned here about how comedy arises out of situation and pathos.

* Day 3: Read Walter Blair's critical history, *Native American Humor*, which is a book about humor that is native to this country and not, as the title leads you to believe, a book of humor by Native Americans.

* Day 4: Listen to (and memorize) George Carlin's "Seven Words You Can't Say on Television." Pay attention to the order of the words and the rhythm that this order creates, and how quite a bit of the humor grows out of the cadence of the list.

* Day 5: Read Charles Portis's novels *Masters of Atlantis* and *Dog of the South*. Portis may be the least-known funniest contemporary American writer.

* Day 6: Watch Triumph, the Insult Comic Dog. Whether you think this is funny or not is a moot point. Watch it. Learn from it.
* Day 7: Memorize an old vaudeville routine (for example, "Who's on First"). Practice it all day long.
* Day 8: Read *The Signet Book of American Humor*, edited by Regina Barreca. How could you go wrong with a book that includes work by both Benjamin Franklin *and* Jeff Foxworthy? Also included are funnyman Henry James and laugh-a-minute Sylvia Plath.
* Day 9: Watch *The Best of Johnny Carson*. And then, by contrast (and as evidence that the end is indeed nigh) watch Jay Leno.
* Day 10: Read up on the Algonquin Round Table then read work by those who were part of it: Dorothy Parker, Robert Benchley, George S. Kaufman, Edna Ferber, etc.
* Day 11: Watch *Saturday Night Live: The Best of Chris Farley*. In particular, watch the skit titled "The Herlihy Boy." If you don't find this funny after the fifth viewing, throw this book away and go back to your day job.
* Day 12: Read *Honey, Hush!: An Anthology of African American Women's Humor*, edited by Daryl Cumber Dance and *Hokum: An Anthology of African American Humor*, edited by Paul Beatty. Granted, I'm asking you to read nearly 2,000 pages in a single day, but so it goes. One must make sacrifices if one wants to become funny.
* Day 13: Work on an impression of someone you know personally but don't like. Hint: The successful impression is really more about nuance than accuracy of voice. A friend of mine believes that in order to do a really good impression, you must either really love the person you're doing an impression of or hate the person. I've come to believe there's a good deal of truth in this.
* Day 14: Spend the entire day watching the Three Stooges. Acceptable combinations of Stooges include "Moe, Larry, and Curly" or "Moe, Larry, and Shemp." Do not, under any circumstance, watch

"Moe, Larry, and Joe" or the feature films starring "Moe, Larry, and Curly-Joe." These are *not* funny.

* Day 15: Take the day off: you may be becoming too funny for your own good. Your less funny friends and neighbors are probably starting to hate you.

* Day 16: Find something in the news and then write a joke about it. This is much harder than you think. Then try it out on your friends, who, if the joke fails, will shun you.

* Day 17: Watch an early Marx Brothers movie, preferably one that includes Zeppo. Zeppo wasn't funny, but the films in which Zeppo appeared are the best Marx Brothers movies. (Quiz: If you can name the elusive *fifth* Marx Brother, you're probably already funny.)

* Day 18: Go to a joke shop and buy a squirting flower or a buzzer that fits in your palm, and then try it out on a colleague. Why is this funny? (You may be the only person laughing, but it *is* funny. Trust me. It is.)

* Day 19: Rent old DVDs of *Rowan and Martin's Laugh-In* but watch only the skits featuring Lily Tomlin. Fast-forward through the rest of it, which isn't funny.

* Day 20: Watch numerous Road Runner cartoons. Notice that the humor is amplified the more we empathize with Wile E. Coyote. After watching the cartoons, read Ian Frazier's brilliant short piece "Coyote v. Acme," which is written in the form of a lawsuit, complete with legalese, in which Coyote sues Acme for the damage he sustained while using their products.

* Day 21: Write a parody of something you see all the time: a personal ad; an author's bio; a memo from work. (Re-read Ian Frazier's "Coyote v. Acme.")

* Day 22: Read short stories by Lorrie Moore, George Saunders, T. C. Boyle, and Sherman Alexie. Compare and contrast.

* Day 23: Time to watch some sitcoms. My recommendations: *The Honeymooners, I Love Lucy, Hogan's Heroes, Sanford and Son,* and

Seinfeld. Pay attention to dialogue and characterization. Ask yourself, who's the straight man (or woman) and who's the comic? Is
there a formula to the configuration of characters? Is Kramer really
just another variation on Sergeant Schultz?

* Day 24: Go up to the top of a building that's at least six stories tall
  and drop a tomato out the window. Why's that funny? Spend the
  rest of the day contemplating this.
* Day 25: Read *The Onion*. If you don't know what *The Onion* is,
  throw this book away and go rent *The Prince of Tides*.
* Day 26: Write a satiric news article in the mode of *The Onion*.
  Good frickin' luck!
* Day 27: Read James Agee's essay, "Comedy's Greatest Era." (Note:
  It's not a funny essay.)
* Day 28: Dust off those old Cheech and Chong albums. Make sure
  they're from the early seventies. Are there any parallels between
  seventies drug humor and the vaudevillians whose sketches you
  memorized? (Are Abbott and Costello really Cheech and Chong's
  kindred spirits?)
* Day 29: Watch the documentary *American Movie*. This movie contains perhaps the funniest moment ever recorded on film. If by the
  end of the movie you're not sure which moment I'm referring to,
  then go back to "Day 1" and start over.
* Day 30: Give this list to your least funny friend, wait thirty days,
  and then see if it works. If it does work, my humor-is-innate theory
  is clearly wrong, and I'm sorry I've wasted your time. If it doesn't,
  I rest my case.

EXERCISES

1. Many of the suggestions above are silly. Or, if not silly, unreason-
   able. But you can find at least two that are doable, so try those
   out. If it's not a writing assignment, write down an analysis of it

afterward. If it's something intended to be funny, was it funny? If so, why? If not, why not?

2. Serious subjects have long been fodder for satire—the lives of prisoners in a German prisoner of war camp in *Hogan's Heroes* or the surgical unit during the Korean War in *M*A*S*H*. (You should note that there is a huge difference between a German prisoner of war camp and a concentration camp, so even if you're going to be irreverent, you should choose your subject matter with care.) For this exercise, choose a subject that's normally reserved for serious exploration (but not necessarily a taboo subject: shock value should *not* be your goal) and write a comic story with the serious subject as the story's centerpiece. Your goal isn't to be offensive or irreverent for the sake of irreverence. Humor is often used as a way to get at the deeper problem that the more serious approach might not be able to touch. In this regard, humor can be quite subversive, and the best humor often is.

3. Write a story in the form of a comic monologue. Your goal: try to make the reader laugh at least every third sentence.

Neighborhoods

WHEN I FIRST began writing fiction, my stories' settings were often amorphous, sometimes nonexistent, or they were rural, probably since I had spent several years living in southern Illinois, where, as an undergraduate, I had decided to become a writer. But it took years for me to be able to write about where I had grown up on the southwest side of Chicago. My first attempts resulted in maudlin prose, and the details I focused on were always gratuitously gritty: the crumbling sidewalks, the bent and twisted guardrails, the broken glass. That sort of thing. But then, in the early nineties, I began writing stories about two characters, Hank and Ralph. Hank was my thirteen-year-old alter ego, and Ralph was based on three different kids I knew when I was growing up, one of whom had failed two years of grade school. The stories almost always grew out of something autobiographical, and once I began using real place names—Ford City Shopping Center; Guidish Park Mobile Homes; the corner of 79th and Narragansett—I finally saw the stories with a clarity that my earlier stories set in nebulous rural towns never achieved.

Granted, I'm a slow learner, but what I eventually discovered was that characters were a product of a place, often a very specific place, and that all place had to do was *be*. Faulkner's books couldn't be set in Anchorage, Alaska, any more than *One Hundred Years of Solitude* could be set in Poughkeepsie. What I discovered was that place provides a context for who people are and why they behave the way they do. The more specific the place, the more intensely those characters become defined because every place has its own urban legends, its own mythologies, and the people who live there have their own peculiar ways, whether it's the food they eat (in my neighborhood, beef sandwiches at Duke's on 85th and Harlem) or the way they insult each other. My characters come from a blue collar background, as do I, and their sensibilities, like my own, are inextricably tied to that socioeconomic environment. In other words, I couldn't simply move the cast of characters in my novel, *The Book of Ralph*, to another location. It wouldn't work. These characters couldn't be from wealthier northern Chicago suburbs, like Winnetka or Evanston, any more than they could be from Mars or the Andromeda Galaxy. Likewise, they couldn't have grown up in the much poorer Cabrini Green housing projects, either. The world they know—the world from which they sprung—is a very specific 4.2-square-mile area, two miles south of Midway Airport, on Chicago's southwest side.

The notion of setting as an essential element of fiction writing isn't new. Pick up any textbook on writing fiction, and you'll find a chapter that will convince you why setting is a good thing. I'd like to go one step further and suggest that you should be thinking about neighborhoods. It's an old-fashioned word that conjures up *The Andy Griffith Show* or, even, *Seinfeld*. And it should. Even though one is set in a small town (Mayberry) and the other in a large city (New York), the characters in both travel in small, intimate circles where they know not only their neighbors but also the people who work in their local businesses, whether it's Floyd the barber or the Soup Nazi, and viewers begin to experience place not in terms of "small town" or "big city" but as something unique to *The Andy Griffith Show* or *Seinfeld*. We *know* those places as well as we know our own neighborhood; maybe we even want to *live* in Mayberry or Seinfeld's New York, even though we know they're fictional. Such is the power of specificity.

In his book *Fiction Writer's Workshop*, Josip Novakovich writes about setting having "fallen out of fashion at the expense of character and action":

> Perhaps this trend has to do with our not being a society of walkers. Big writers used to be big walkers. Almost every day, Honoré de Balzac spent hours strolling the streets of Paris; Charles Dickens, the streets of London; Fyodor Dostoyevski, the streets of St. Petersburg. Their cities speak out from them.

If Novakovich's assertion that place has fallen out of fashion is correct, I suspect one reason is because the country itself has become less and less distinct—the same shopping malls; the same gas stations; the same Wal-Marts and K-marts. How many times have I, after arriving in an unfamiliar city, walked into a Target that is laid out exactly like the Target in my own city and then, after shopping under the familiar fluorescent lighting, walked outside only to have no idea where I was? In the 1980s, there was a trend in fiction to capture the fact that every place in modern America was just like every other place (Frederick Barthelme's stories that appeared in the *New Yorker* probably captured this best), but there was also a backlash to this kind of fiction right around the time Richard Russo's first novel *Mohawk*, featuring an individually-owned diner, appeared in 1986. Kent Haruf has also had quite a bit of success with novels set in tiny Holt, Colorado, where you would be hard-pressed to find a Blockbuster or McDonald's. These are writers whose settings are neighborhoods with clearly defined boundaries and populations with recurring characters—in short, places that are distinctly their own and not interchangeable with another writer's setting.

Even in a city as large as Chicago, for instance, Stuart Dybek says, "For me, what would typify Chicago writers is an interest in neighborhood, and in immigration, and in ethnicity. This is a city where everyone asks you, 'What are you?' The answer is never 'American.'" What Dybek says is absolutely true. For the Chicago writers I know, the "city" isn't a single monolithic entity. Instead, they write about neighborhoods that are distinctly different from each other. Joe Meno's southwest side is Evergreen Park. My southwest side is a few miles north, in Burbank. They may be similar, but they're not the same. Stuart Dybek writes about Chicago's Pilsen neighborhood while Billy Lombardo writes of Bridgeport. Stephanie Kuehnert writes about the underbelly of Oak Park. Furthermore, neighborhoods are a moveable feast, which is to say that the Burbank I write primarily about (Burbank of the 1970s) isn't the Burbank of today. Dybek's Pilsen of the 1950s and 60s no longer exists. So, two writers writing about the same neighborhood will likely be writing about two distinctly different places depending on where they fall on that neighborhood's timeline.

In this regard, it may be best to think of your fiction on a very specific time-place continuum. I recently read a novel set, in part, in Lincoln, Nebraska, a city where I spent a little over four years in the 1990s. There was absolutely nothing in the novel to suggest that the author had ever even stepped foot in Lincoln, let alone done any research or lived there. The result was that I didn't believe the book at all. It's the difference between hearsay and tangible evidence. Which is more compelling in a trial? In a novel or story, the author can tell me that a character lives in Lincoln, Nebraska, but if she doesn't present anything tangible for the reader, why should I believe any of it?

The best way to achieve universality is through specificity. In other words, if you give your story or novel a generic setting, readers won't say, "Ah, yes, I can superimpose my own stores and street names and schools here, and it'll be just like some place I know." The only way to get the reader to begin making connections between the fictional world you've created and his life is to be specific. *Very* specific. This may seem counterintuitive, but generic settings remain fuzzy whereas detailed settings often trigger something specific in the reader's memory—a place he used to shop with his mother, the school where he attended kindergarten, a barbershop he drove by many years ago and had forgotten all about until he saw it here in this book, even though it's not the same barbershop and even though it's not even in the same state. After my novel *The Book of Ralph* was released, I received numerous e-mails that began, "I know this is odd, but I thought you were writing about where I grew up in . . ." Plug in the city. The e-mails came from people living in Kansas, New Mexico, Connecticut, and elsewhere. Obviously, I *wasn't* writing about where they grew up, but something about the specificity in that book allowed certain readers to recall something from their own pasts. I hadn't planned this; I'm not that smart. It wasn't until after the book was published that I slowly began to realize the power of specificity in regard to place and its effect on readers.

What I didn't realize, either, was that setting would play an important role in my readership and, later, in the marketing of my book. People love to read about where they're from, and since I was writing about actual places, sometimes places that no longer existed, such as the Sheridan Drive-in on the corner of 79th and Harlem, I attracted readers who weren't necessarily readers of literary fiction but who, for one reason or another, found out about the book and decided to read it for reasons having more to do with nostalgia—the romanticization of place. Many of the e-mails I received after the book came out were from people who had grown up where the book was set and who wanted to ask me if I remembered this place or that. At book signings and readings I give on Chicago's southwest side, the people who show up often want to talk not about my books but about our old neighborhood. At one event at my hometown library, after I had read a short chapter set in the Ford City Shopping Center that mentions how bomber planes were built there during World War II, an elderly woman in the front row began talking about how she had worked on one of those assembly lines in the 1940s, and then she described the place and populated it for us to see. She was staking out her territory, saying to all of us, "Look, this was once mine."

I staked out my place by accident, but by doing so, I tapped into an audience I hadn't anticipated—my fellow southwest siders. One of my favorite reviews of the book, which echoes in slightly different language e-mails I've received, appears from a reader on Goodreads. She wrote, "The main reason I like this book so much is the author is from my home town and most of it is set there. This guy really captured the feeling of that shitty little place and reminded me why I love and hate Burbank."

What better compliment could a writer ask for?

EXERCISES

---

1. Pick a notable intersection where you grew up. By "notable," I mean one that was notable for you personally. For me, it was 79th and Narragansett in Burbank, Illinois. Where was it for you? Now, re-

create it on the page as vividly as you can. Work from photos, if you have any. Try to fill in as much detail as possible. Ask people who know that intersection for their memories. You may be surprised by what you've forgotten. Don't think in terms of story. This is a sketch, a memory, a restoration. When you're done, consider writing a story in which this setting is important, if not essential.

2. Pick a historical location. By "historical," I don't necessarily mean famous. Also, be sure that your location is specific and contained rather than generic (for example, Paris) and sprawling. Also, be sure it's a place you can research, by either looking at photos or reading about it. (While doing research for a novel set in 1871, I found in a photograph a place called Col. Wood's Museum. The longer I looked at the photo, the more intrigued I became. I eventually tracked down more information about the place, and although there wasn't a lot to be found, there was enough to make the place an important location in my novel.) After doing research, write a sketch of the place. After writing a sketch, make a list of three characters that might have populated this place. Who are they, and what would they have been doing there?

3. Sometimes, a confined space can create a tremendous amount of tension. In Alfred Hitchcock's movie *Lifeboat*, a group of people try to survive on a lifeboat, even as tensions mount between them. Or think of the Jodie Foster movie *Panic Room*. Although not entirely restricted to one setting, as *Lifeboat* is, much of the movie takes place in a single room. For this exercise, write a very short story (five to eight pages) set in a confined space. You may want first to think carefully about what this confined space looks like, what its exact dimensions are, and what, if any, objects are in it before writing the actual story.

The Imitative Fallacy

T HE IMITATIVE FALLACY is when a writer attempts to mirror the narrator's state of mind through some aspect of craft (prose, structure, plot, etc.). The drunker the narrator, the less coherent the prose becomes. The "crazier" the narrator, the less lucid the story's structure becomes. The more mentally-challenged the narrator, the harder it becomes to follow what's happening in the story.

Beginning writers are drawn to the imitative fallacy to the point that it's become a cliché. The appeal is that it's clever, but as I pointed out elsewhere in this book, accuracy is harder—and ultimately more rewarding—than cleverness, cleverness being often obvious and, because it's overdone, not at all original. The student may argue, "But I want the reader to experience what the narrator is experiencing." Unfortunately, the opposite usually happens: the reader is reminded that there is an author manipulating the prose and, as a result, feels less inside the narrator's head, not more. As I often ask my students, would you want to read a story about the world's most boring guy written in the world's most boring prose? Of course not.

Perhaps a case can be made for the imitative fallacy in first person present-tense stories, which would make logical sense because we would be inside the narrator's head during the most immediate moment possible, but I would likely suggest using a different point of view or a different tense so as to avoid the imitative fallacy altogether.

The most familiar logical fallacy story I run across is what I'll call the "crazy narrator story." The plots I've seen dozens of times are remarkably similar. A narrator slips into insanity, but the insanity is often withheld from the reader. Instead, we pick up on the narrator's insanity through the weird thoughts the narrator has or by the incoherence of the prose. In almost all of these stories, the "craziness" is generic, most likely inspired by TV or movies rather than any actual personal experience or serious research on the subject. Is the narrator manic depressive, schizophrenic, or a sociopath? Whenever I ask for an actual diagnosis, the author shrugs or says, "I don't know." This is a problem. I'm not suggesting that the writer needs to have experienced her own descent into madness in order to write effectively about it, only that one type of mental illness isn't interchangeable with another one, and if the author wants the reader to really, truly believe in what she's writing, the writer needs to acknowledge the complexity of mental illness and portray it in a way that's more credible than it's portrayed in nearly every story where the imitative fallacy is employed.

I tend to believe that the more a narrator's consciousness is impaired (by booze, by drugs, by a low IQ, by mental problems), the harder the writer needs to work in the opposite direction so as not to lose her reader. In other words: the less lucid the narrator, the more lucid the prose. While writing his novel *Disturbing the Peace*, much of which inhabited the mind of a character who would slip into periods of full-blown mania, Richard Yates told an interviewer, "What I'd like to do is have the man go crazy without letting the book go crazy." In other words, Yates wanted to avoid the imitative fallacy, and he did. The result is a novel with extraordinarily chilling moments. Midway through the novel, after John Wilder, the novel's main character, has recovered and is on the set of a movie being made about his time spent in a psychiatric hospital, he begins to have another breakdown shortly after a discussion by cast members and crew of the virtues of a scene depicting the film's John Wilder character as a Christ figure. Wilder, who leaves the film set, goes for a walk in the woods. His thoughts become somewhat less lucid, but Yates never lets the reader lose grounding with reality. On the same page that Wilder's thoughts become stranger, Wilder passes a minor actor in the woods, and the actor says, "You okay, Mr. Wilder? You look—"

"How do I look?"

"I don't know." And the boy lowered his eyes like a girl. "No special way, I guess; I just—never mind. By the way, I think it's a great film, Mr. Wilder. Really great."

This is the reader's cue that Wilder is having another manic episode, which allows us to see vividly into Wilder's mind without ever being confused as to what's going on. Shortly after the scene with the minor actor, Yates presents us with a paragraph that, without the previous scene, probably wouldn't make much sense:

> He didn't want to look up because he knew the sky had turned from blue to red and yellow, and he didn't want to look back because Pamela and all the young men were gathered there under the massed trees to urge him on—keep going, John; keep going—so he looked down at his own walking feet. These were the feet that had taken him through years and years of error and falsehood; now they were treading the dirt of the right road at last—the true road, the high, lonely road of self-discovery.

Wilder meets up with yet another member of the film, who, after speaking to Wilder for a moment, expresses a similar concern to that of the minor actor:

> Epstein's smile had given way to a troubled look, but his hand was still there and Wilder shook it.
>
> "You're—all right, aren't you, Mr. Wilder?"

Once again, the characters whose points of view we're not privy to are the ones who provide us with the perspective (the *sane* perspective) that we need to accurately interpret what's happening in this scene. It should also be noted that Yates doesn't gratuitously extend this scene. Two pages later, John Wilder is being cared for in a hospital.

Whenever you give up something as a writer (the narrator's lucidity, sanity, or intelligence), you have to figure out a way to compensate for it. In writing—as is often the case in life—the path of least resistance usually leads to fewer gains. If you're giving up your narrator's IQ points, you'd better write the smartest story anyone has ever read. If I want to spend thirty minutes with an unintelligible, rambling drunk, I'll go to a bar; I won't read a short story with prose that's rambling—and, no, it's *not* stream of consciousness. It's just sprawling, undisciplined writing. It's easy to write rambling prose; it's harder—much harder—to capture accurately a drunk's state of mind in coherent prose.

A real problem with the imitative fallacy is that it takes something like mental illness and, by turning it into a clever plot devise, trivializes it. Yes, one of fiction's functions is to entertain, and, yes, movies and books have a long history of exploiting serious issues for the sake of entertainment, but I don't believe entertaining the reader and dealing with a serious subject in an honest way are mutually exclusive.

Numerous writers have tackled these complex subjects in novels and short stories without resorting to imitative fallacies. Sylvia Plath's brilliant novel *The Bell Jar* captures a young woman's descent into clinical depression without succumbing to gloomy prose. If anything, Plath's prose and plot remain lively, oftentimes humorous, throughout.

The first person narrator of Jonathan Lethem's novel *Motherless Brooklyn* has Tourette's, but the book's narration (the narration being the parts of the book that aren't dialogue) doesn't devolve into a barrage of profanity and insults, which is what the writer committing the imitative fallacy would have done. On having a hard-boiled detective narrator with Tourette's, Lethem told *Post Road*:

> Of course I found it incredibly funny, snort-milk-through-the-nose funny. I still do. As much as I've invested in Lionel and his Tourette's —and he's obviously the character I've written with whom I most identify —it all starts with wanting to do this funny, stupid, seemingly impossible thing. Subsequently, I layered over the potential affront of how funny I wanted to be with all kinds of intricate sensitivity to the real-world suffering of Touretters and their loved ones.

It's an affliction—in the lives of sufferers and their families often a terrible one. And the world is terribly insensitive. I didn't want to add to that even slightly. I hope I haven't. But the book in fact thrived on this struggle to have things both ways—my awkward negotiation translated to the reader, I think, so that it becomes a very emotional book, very emotionally open.

Two things Lethem says here are telling. The first is that Lionel, the novel's narrator, is the character, of all the characters Lethem has created, with whom he most identifies. It would be extraordinarily difficult, if not impossible, to identify with a character that you didn't empathize with, and empathy may be the paramount factor in making stories like this one work.

The second notable quote is that Lethem didn't in any way want to be insensitive to the families of those afflicted. Would a writer writing a point of view character with Tourette's for the sake of cleverness alone express such a sentiment? Probably not. Having said that, I concede that some readers will still be offended by the premise alone, but, as I've noted elsewhere in this book, no writer can please everyone. The best a writer can do is approach his characters with empathy and treat the subject matter with honesty.

There are novels that may, by synopses alone, appear to be guilty of the imitative fallacy, when in fact these authors are performing a kind of sleight of hand. They are doing the seemingly impossible, conveying the narrator's state of mind through the prose (or some other narrative device) while remaining accessible to the reader. It's as though these authors are two places at once: inside the narrator's head *and* hovering above the scene.

One such novel is *Lowboy* by John Wray. *Lowboy* is the story of Will Heller, a sixteen-year-old paranoid schizophrenic. The opening of the novel is written in a series of short paragraphs from Heller's third person point of view. Some of Heller's thoughts are lucid (we know, for instance, that he's on a train), but some are cryptic ("The floor was shivering and ticking beneath his feet and the bricktiled arches above the train beat the murmurings of the crowd into copper and aluminum foil."). But as early as the second page, the perspective shifts for a paragraph into the omniscient point of view of the people on the train, and the story jumps into the future: "Everyone in the car would later agree that the boy seemed in very high spirits." By the paragraph's end, the reader has been clued in that something isn't right with the boy: "What's a boy like that doing, a few of them wondered, dressed in such hideous clothes?" The second chapter introduces the point of view of a police detective who specializes in missing persons. We are also introduced to Will Heller's mother in this chapter. In short, the reader is not confined to Will Heller's altered perspective. By offering the reader other perspectives, a context is provided for Will Heller's thoughts. It quickly becomes clear that this novel isn't an exercise in seeing how long its author can sustain a gimmick. And the point of the novel isn't for the reader to come to the epiphany that the narrator is a paranoid schizophrenic. If that were the case, the novel wouldn't rise above being a joke with a punch line. And no one would be interested in re-reading a three hundred page joke, especially not more than once. It's worth reinforcing, though, that this is a novel, not a short story. Such shifts in perspectives in a short story would only highlight the gimmick and exacerbate the problem.

On occasion, the form of the story may inspire the writer toward the imitative fallacy, but, as with all of the other examples in this chapter, the better writer sidesteps the obvious and, instead, honors the power of character and story. One such story is "Free Writing" by Sondra Spatt Olsen, which uses a series of free writing exercises as the story's form. For those who aren't familiar with a free writing exercise, it's a technique used in writing courses to get students to write something, anything, without them lifting their pen from page with the hope that they will break through to some writing of significance. As you can imagine, a story using free writing as a form could easily devolve into rambling nonsense or stream of consciousness jibber-jabber. The skilled writer realizes that you have to give the *illusion* that the entries are actually the character's free writing without losing sight that there's a story to be told, which is precisely what Sandra Spatt Olsen deftly accomplishes.

Olsen's narrator teaches composition, and the conceit of the story is that she's writing free writing exercises along with her class. At first, there is a rambling quality to the prose that might approximate an actual free writing exercise, but we quickly learn the source of the narrator's tension in her life, and as the story progresses, the entries turn into full-blown, dramatized scenes. Had Olsen been faithful to the form, which would have been a mistake, the entire story would have rambled on, jumping from thought to thought without much logic and with no concern for story or character development. The free writing entries provide a framework for Olsen that, in turn, allows her to convey the passing of the semester. The structure is clever, but Olsen doesn't use cleverness as a crutch.

Perhaps the best example of this sleight of hand is Mark Haddon's novel *The Curious Incident of the Dog in the Night-time*, the story of Christopher John Francis Boone, a fifteen-year-old boy with autism who attempts to solve the mystery of his neighbor's murdered dog. Flip through the book without reading it, and you'll see charts, graphs, puzzles, drawings of shapes, math problems, floor plans, and a variety of other odd things you're not likely to find in a traditional novel. The book *looks* overly clever. But once you begin to read the book, it becomes immediately clear that Haddon isn't interested in sacrificing story for cleverness. The point of all the drawings in this book isn't simply to recreate Christopher's state of mind. Yes, they do give us insight into how Christopher *thinks*, but the drawings are always in service of the larger story, Christopher's journey to discover who murdered the neighbor's dog, which, in turn, opens up a Pandora's Box that's full of secrets about Christopher's own life. Haddon's accomplishment throughout this book is that, yes, we do get a glimpse into Christopher's logic—why he says and does things that are often inexplicable to others—but we also understand the frustrations of those around him, because we see their reactions (in all likelihood, we would react similarly), and we understand why they can't penetrate Christopher's logic, even as we're privy to it. It's a remarkable accomplishment for a novelist to achieve, the ability to put the reader in a variety of places all at the same time through a single point of view.

The imitative fallacy story that uses autism would be mercilessly internal with no larger goal than making the reader guess what's going on: "Ah ha! I get it! The narrator is autistic!" (I've seen such stories presented to workshops, and their authors sometimes become smug when other readers are confused or can't identify the narrator's affliction, as though the story itself is a test and the narrator's symptoms have been dramatized for the purpose of quizzing its readers.)

As with every rule in this book, there will be exceptions. Perhaps the best-known exception to this rule—the novel that comes closest to committing the imitative fallacy and getting away with it—is *Flowers for Algernon* by Daniel Keyes, the story of, among other things, the first human test subject for surgery to increase intelligence. The novel is, in part, structured around a series of progress reports by Charlie, whose limited intelligence is evident in the heading of his very first report: "progris riport 1 martch 3." During the course of the novel, Charlie becomes more intelligent and more articulate, and the prose on the page becomes more and more sophisticated. In this regard, the novel is a twist on the imitative fallacy in that it moves from a state of impairment to a state of clarity, and the bulk of the novel is written in the latter state, thereby eliminating most of the problems associated with the logical fallacy. Furthermore, the novel is technically science fiction, which gives the author more latitude in regard to what he chooses to do with the genre's conventions. By this, I mean that the imitative fallacy has long been a trope of science fiction. (There are numerous early horror stories, for instance, with narrators that go insane.) As such, Keyes was working within a certain tradition while doing something new with it. While *Flowers for Algernon* may be a novel that employs the imitative fallacy, it both mitigates common problems normally associated with the imitative fallacy and transcends the imitative fallacy by being more than just a clever exercise meant to surprise the reader.

EXERCISES

----

1. Make a list of other potential imitative fallacies. Are any of these good subjects to write about without resorting to the imitative fallacy?

2. Write three pages of a story in which you consistently commit a logical fallacy. Next, write three pages of the same story in which you avoid the logical fallacy. (For the second part of this assignment, you'll probably want to do some research, unless you already have knowledge about the thing—whatever that thing may be—that would cause a writer to commit the logical fallacy in the first place.)

3. In "Free Writing," Sondra Spatt Olsen uses the form of a free writing exercise to structure her story. As noted in this chapter, she could easily have allowed the story to fall into the imitative fallacy trap by accurately mimicking free writing exercises at the expense of story and characterization. For this exercise, choose an established form (a legal document, directions to operate a piece of machinery, a university's bylaws, etc.) and then write a story using the form you've chosen as the story's structure but without falling prey to the imitative fallacy.

Subtext

I F I WERE TO SIT DOWN and calculate how long it sometimes takes me to write a short story from conception to final draft, I would probably quit writing altogether. And yet I begin each project optimistically, naively thinking that I understand what the story is about, when in fact I know virtually *nothing* about the story and may not know anything about it for years.

It's taken me a long time to realize what revision is all about—that is, what it's about for me. It's about discovering the story's subtext. The story always has a surface story, the obvious thing that the story is about, but what does all of it mean? How do the disparate elements of a story add up to mean something that's greater than its individual parts? What's the story's cumulative effect?

The story's text is what the story's about, but the story's subtext is what the story's *really* about. Here's what I believe: the conscious mind is what's piecing together the obvious story; the unconscious mind, working much as it does with dreams, tries subverting the obvious story by dropping in the surprising detail, the jarring line of dialogue, the unexpected guest, the unsettling turn of events. *Why does this shoe horn keep showing up in the story? Why did Phil mouth off? Who invited Mary Beth to come over just then? And why did the next door neighbor park his car in his neighbor's driveway instead of his own?* You think you're in control of your story, but the truth is, you're not. It's my belief that while the unconscious mind is wreaking havoc on your quiet, domestic story, it's also feeding you the subtext. The subtext, as I suggested above, is the story's dream world, and since you rarely know in real life why you dream about the things you do, the story's subtext also takes time and distance (in both *your* life and the *story's* life) for its meaning to become clear.

If the story itself is a lake, then its subtext is the Loch Ness monster, dipping in and out, keeping mostly hidden, but sometimes rising up and scaring the bejesus out of you. Or sometimes the subtext is the main story's doppelgänger: it looks like the main story, it has the same cast of characters, but it's acting in peculiar ways, and (more frighteningly) it has its own agenda, separate from your own.

Revision is the act of teasing the Loch Ness monster out of the water or drawing the doppelgänger out from the shadows so that we can take a good look, see it more clearly, and perhaps understand why it's doing what it's doing. Once we finally understand its purpose, the subtext comes into focus and then the story as a whole (after more revision, of course) becomes spherical instead of merely round. The story becomes an experience for the reader rather than mere words on a page. As Flannery O'Connor said about successful short stories, two plus two is always greater than four. Why? The answer is subtext.

A REVISION WILL TAKE ME anywhere from one to six years. (See chapter "Gestation" for more on the importance of allowing a piece of writing to evolve over time.) Fortunately, I work on several projects at once—a revolving stack of stories, novels, and screenplays—otherwise I'd be the least productive writer working today. I tend to write first drafts quickly, so I'm not a slow writer. I am, however, a slow learner, and every year I'll come to some realization about fiction writing that would have made my life a hell of a lot easier if it had dawned on me twenty years ago.

Learning how to revise a story came to me slowly, and it wasn't until I'd been writing seriously for nine years that it finally clicked. Until then, I'd thought revision was all about finding the right words, working on pacing, varying syntax, and so on—and it is about all of those things, but all of those things should be in the service of figuring out what the story is really about. This finally occurred to me while working on two different stories. One was a loosely autobiographical story about a man who, after a startlingly brief marriage, was starting to drink too much and, as a result, misinterpret the things happening around him. The other story was a purely fictional story about a man named Roger who was obsessed with Charles Manson and the Manson Family. Neither story was working. The first had no plot; the second had no character motivation. One was too real; the other was too outlandish. One day, I had the two stories side by side, trying to figure out which one to work on when I noticed similarities between them. The narrators were eerily similar; the general mood of each story was similar as well. There was one striking difference. One story (the autobiographical story) was primarily external; I rarely entered the narrator's head. The other story was almost entirely internal. It was as if I had split one character in two, divvying up point-of-view strategies: this character sees the world while that character thinks about it. Side by side, I realized that the two stories were really talking to each other. One was succumbing to the darkness of his own life; the other was embracing the darkness. It wasn't easy putting the two stories together. I had to cut a lot from each story, including some of my favorite passages, but it was necessary because these two stories were meant to be together. The realization that they belonged together was more exciting than any realization I'd had as a fiction writer up until that point. I felt like Dr. Frankenstein patching together something living from something dead. And like Dr. Frankenstein, I had created something scarier than I had anticipated, something that took on a life separate from me, a story that began to tell me what it was all about rather than the other way around.

That particular story was a personal and artistic catharsis for me. I don't write fiction for therapy, and I tend to believe that if you go into writing a story with the hope of healing yourself, the story will seem too obvious and the reader will likely be embarrassed for you. But I do believe that every story that comes truly and fully alive is, in truth, a form of personal catharsis. The kicker is that you're usually the last to realize it.

To some extent, our relationship to our own stories is that of an analyst to her patient. Our job is to meet regularly with our patient (the story) with the hope that each session will bring about a series of illuminations that lead, ultimately, to an epiphany. We may need to meet for only a month or two, but sometimes we meet for years. Occasionally, we never stop meeting. These are the stories that we haven't given up hope on but that never seem to work. I tend to believe that such a story suffers from one of two problems: it has a subtext that's so personal that we may never have enough distance to figure out what it means, or it has no subtext at all, in which case revising the story is like chasing a mirage. Without a subtext, the story will never materialize; it'll never turn to flesh and blood. Sadly, these are the ones we probably cling to the longest when we should really just let them go.

- -

YOU'D THINK I'D HAVE figured out a faster way to detect the story's subtext after spending over twenty years in this game, but I haven't. I recently started writing what I thought would be a short-short. It was to be no longer than five pages. As of today, it's eighteen pages with no end in sight. The story has gone in several unexpected directions, and characters I hadn't fathomed when I began writing have barged into the story, disrupting what was supposed to be a straightforward narrative.

Do I know yet what the story is about? Not really. Not yet, at least.

Do I know yet how long the story will take to write? Not a clue.

Will I continue working on it? Absolutely. As writers, this is as close as we get to unlocking the secrets to our own odd and mysterious lives. How could I possibly turn my back on that?

EXERCISES
----

1. What moments in your life took a good amount of time for you
   to realize the full import of them? Is there an example from childhood? What about one from adulthood?

2. This may or may not result in a story worth keeping, but try writing a story the moment you wake up (yes, you can brush your teeth,
   but, no, you can't check e-mail), and try to write the entire story
   in one sitting. Write quickly. Then take a look at what surprised
   you. Where did the story take unexpected twists? What characters
   showed up with no more than a few seconds' notice? How is this
   story different from ones you normally write?

3. Read over one of your completed stories. What's *not* being said?
   What's the story hinting at? What's the story really about . . . or
   trying to be about? If you were to tease it out subtly, how would you
   go about it? What threads would you pull on? What scenes would
   you rewrite? Would you eliminate any characters so as to heighten
   the potential subtext? Would you add any?

Gestation

I USED TO THINK that there was a logical way to write and revise a story. Why wouldn't there be? You sit down and hammer out a story, and then you take it through several drafts. Eventually, the story comes together or it doesn't. If it does, it's finished. If it doesn't, you discard it . . . or you send it to magazines anyway and hope no one notices that it doesn't work. Sounds simple.

What I've come to learn is that the final drafts of my short stories and novels are rarely the end result of a logical process. Oh, sure, occasionally a story will follow the pattern above, but more often than not it doesn't.

I tend to think that every piece of fiction has a gestation period during which the story or novel needs time to percolate in the writer's head in order for it to make sense to her, but the problem is that the writer has no idea how long that gestation period is going to be. This is why some short stories have taken me as long as six years to write. (Most short stories don't take six years, but a few have taken that long because I needed time to figure it all out, to connect the seemingly random dots, where plot and meaning finally merge together.)

All of my novels, despite the actual time spent writing them, have had long gestation periods. My first novel, *The Book of Ralph*, was written mostly over a two-year period before the book's publication, between 2001 and 2003, and if someone asks me how long it took to write, I tell them two years because that's the easiest answer to give. In truth, the origins of the book can be traced back to the spring of 1993 when I wrote a short story titled "The Backyard." It was a failure, so I completely reconfigured "The Backyard" later that summer, keeping only a dog named Tex and one particular image from the story. I created an entirely new cast of characters, all of whom eventually became the central cast of *The Book of Ralph*. The new story was titled "Smoke," and it appeared in a small magazine a year after I wrote it. Over the next three years, from 1993 to 1996, I wrote two more "Ralph" short stories. All three of these eventually appeared in my story collection *Troublemakers*, published in 2000. I had toyed with writing a few more "Ralph" stories with the idea of including them in another future collection, but three things happened. The first was that the new "Ralph" stories were unwieldy, and I found myself dividing each story into two stories. Clearly, the material I was working with was too large for the container of an individual short story. The second thing was that *Troublemakers* had been published, and the reviews were almost unanimous in their support of the "Ralph" stories as the book's strongest pieces, which, in turn, energized me to work harder on these new stories. The third thing was that I had written three unsuccessful novels by 2002, so the idea of writing a book constructed entirely out of short stories appealed to me. (I should note that the book, while technically a novel-in-stories, was eventually marketed as a novel.) Although I tell people it took two years to write *The Book of Ralph*, the more truthful, accurate answer is that it took closer to ten years.

The evolution of my second novel, *America's Report Card*, was stranger. *America's Report Card* is a darkly comic novel about, among other things, the standardized testing industry. I have worked, off and on, in this industry, either writing tests or scoring them. I took my first scoring job in the late 1990s when I couldn't find any other work. It was a truly miserable job, and what I witnessed on a daily basis convinced me that the entire industry was corrupt. I began taking notes with the idea that I would eventually write an essay that I might pitch to *Harper's*, but when I told my then-agent that I had signed a confidentiality agreement, she told me I couldn't write the essay, that I would open myself up to lawsuits. I tried writing three or four pages of fiction set in the world of standardized testing, but I couldn't figure out how to make it work, so I put all of my notes inside a shoebox and set it aside. But something was there; I could feel it. Occasionally, I would open the shoebox, pick through it, and read over the notes, but then

I would set it aside again. Fast-forward to 2005: I was trying to write the second book of a two-book contract, but my first idea kept dying. (This is precisely why I don't like writing fiction under contract: it doesn't allow for a gestation period, which, for me, is perhaps the most important aspect of the process.) With the proposed novel dying in front of me, I began mulling over other ideas. Once again, I opened the shoebox—eight years after I had written most of the notes—and I began to see ways that I could make the novel work. Partly, it had to do with the times we were living in: post-9/11; two wars; a deeply divided nation. The world had changed quite a bit during those eight years, and the tone that I wanted for this material—paranoid and conspiratorial—made better sense now than it did when I first took those notes. The times we lived in had caught up to the weirdness of the material I had been saving. In other words, what seemed far-fetched eight years earlier was now perfectly credible.

My third novel, *After the Workshop*, was written quickly in 2008. Early that year, I had been visiting New York, having dinner with my then-agent, telling her anecdotes of when I had been a media escort for authors. She perked up and said, "You should write that book!" I asked if I should write it as nonfiction or fiction. "Fiction," she said. "Definitely fiction." Back home, I started working on a satire on the book industry, testing it out to see if it kept my interest. Three months later, I was done with a first draft. Seven months after our conversation, I had completed the book. The subject had broadened so that it was now a satire that included everything having to do with writing—writing workshops, publicity, even author's jacket photos. Everything was fair game. I had lived in this world and knew it intimately. I didn't need to live with this material. For all practical purposes, I *was* the novel's narrator. After writing the book, a memory had come to me: hadn't I tried writing this book once before? I went to my basement and opened a filing cabinet drawer, and sure enough, there it was: *Murder at the Writers' Workshop*. Right after I had graduated from the Iowa Writers' Workshop in 1989, I had hammered out fifty or so pages of a comic murder mystery set in the world of the creative writing workshop and featuring all the archetypes you'd likely encounter there. As I skimmed the pages, I realized that versions of the same characters appeared in both pieces of writing. Even some of the scenes were eerily similar, even though I hadn't looked at *Murder at the Writers' Workshop* since I'd filed it away nearly twenty years earlier. Clearly, the material had been gestating in my subconscious, but I was probably too close to the subject matter in 1989 to write effectively about it. It took almost two decades and another person's suggestion for me to return to it, and the speed at which I wrote that novel suggests that the material was already there, fully formed, waiting to be released.

NO PROJECT OF MINE has had a more curious history than a short story titled "The Phone Call."

I need to provide some backstory first. The backstory is about my mother's death, which I've never written about directly. (See chapter "The Ideal Reader" for more about the connection between my mother and my work.) My mother had had very little formal education (she left school after graduating from eighth grade) and had a particularly difficult work life (a child of sharecroppers, she had learned to pick cotton at three years old; as an adult, she worked mostly on factory assembly-lines). She was a smart woman who was limited by the circumstances of her life—extreme poverty as a child and a soul-killing blue-collar adult life. She didn't have many options. But she was a gifted oral storyteller, and I spent a great deal of my childhood listening to her stories, no doubt unconsciously picking up *how* to tell a story by paying attention to her. I was extraordinarily close to my mother, and we often sat across from each other at the kitchen table, psychoanalyzing people we knew, trying to figure out what made them tick. She would drink coffee and smoke. She smoked Winstons. She smoked four packs of Winstons a day. Some days she would light a cigarette even as another smoldered in an adjoining room, forgotten. When she was fifty-two years old, she was diagnosed with lung cancer.

I was an undergraduate in college, a senior, when she was diagnosed. The summer before she was diagnosed, I had come home for a while, sleeping on the couch, and my mother would get up in the middle of the night from coughing fits. She was coughing up blood, but she was in denial, as was I, of what the blood portended.

Eventually, my mother did see a doctor. She suffered through a brutal operation that accomplished nothing because the cancer had spread from her lung to her aorta. Initially, she was given three months to live, but an experimental treatment kept her alive for two more years.

I was in my second year of graduate school when she died. The day before she died, I had driven back to Chicago to be with her. As I sat with her the next morning, the time between her breaths grew longer and longer, and then, shortly after two P.M., there were no more breaths. I waited. I held her hand and brushed her hair with my palm. Nothing. She had been conscious that morning when I had first arrived, but for the previous four hours she hadn't been, and at one point I had whispered to her that it was okay, that she could go now, but after she died I was furious at myself for telling her it was okay. I wasn't ready for her to go. Of *course* it wasn't okay. What had I been thinking?

I remained with her body for over an hour. I waited for something extraordinary to happen—I wasn't sure what—but nothing happened. I remember thinking, *All these amazing stories . . . everything she knew, her entire history . . . it's gone now, all of it.*

This was December of 1988. For the first six months after her death, I was grief-stricken. And then one night I had a dream. Except that it didn't feel like a dream. It was of my mother leaning over me as I slept, reaching down and taking hold of my arm, and saying, "Everything's okay. Don't worry about me. I'm fine." Her grasp on my hand felt like someone actually holding my arm as I slept, and when I woke up I felt better. More at peace. The bad dreams—dreams of my mother buried alive, for instance—stopped. I'm not someone who puts much stock in the supernatural, and I'm not by any means religious. I'm not going to speculate about what happened because whatever it was—even if it was my own brain working hard to give me closure, as I tend to believe it most likely was—it worked.

Sort of.

One year later, during my first teaching job, I woke up in the middle of the night, walked to my typewriter, and began hammering out a short story. I wrote the entire story in one sitting. It was titled "The Phone Call," and the basic premise was of a man who, after a night of drinking, calls his old childhood phone number on a whim, and his mother, who had died many years earlier, picks up the phone. He talks to her for a while but keeps getting disconnected. Each time he calls, time has jumped forward. Also, each time he calls, he can hear his mother lighting a cigarette to smoke. He begins begging her to stop smoking, but the phone calls grow shorter and shorter, and his mother never addresses his concerns. Eventually, the phone number has been disconnected. In the end, there is nothing the narrator can do to turn back time and save his mother.

The story, such as it was, was clearly a forum for me to work out my own guilt. I could have tried to get my own mother to stop smoking, but would I have been able to convince her of the outcome to have made her quit?

I printed up a copy of "The Phone Call," and then an odd thing happened. I lost it. Now, I'm a pack rat. I never lose anything. I still have drafts of stories I wrote when I was an undergraduate. But this story—"The Phone Call"—disappeared. It was as though I had dreamed it all.

For years afterward, I considered rewriting the story. Objectively, I wasn't crazy about the autobiographical stuff, but I liked the premise—the basic idea of someone, via the phone, connecting with his past and trying to change the outcome. I occasionally jotted some notes. When I began writing screenplays, I wondered if this could work as one and began outlining it, but talking on a phone is visually static, and I couldn't figure out a way around it. I decided that it might work as a short movie—ten or fifteen minutes long—but I wasn't a filmmaker, I was a writer, so the idea of writing a screenplay for something that most likely would never get made didn't interest me.

Somewhere around 2002, I found my copy of "The Phone Call." The paper had yellowed, and the ink from the dot-matrix printer had faded some, but the story was intact. I read the first page but decided not to read any more of it. I didn't want to be influenced by the original version should

I ever decide to rework it, so I set it aside. I haven't seen it since. I looked for it recently, out of curiosity, but couldn't find it.

In 2011, I was contacted by Ray Bradbury's friend and biographer, the writer Sam Weller, about contributing a story to an anthology of stories inspired by the work of Bradbury. Contributors would include Margaret Atwood, Neil Gaiman, and Alice Hoffman, among others. Would I care to contribute a story? Of course!

At first, I wrote down a few vague ideas, but I didn't feel ready to write them. I started re-reading some early Bradbury stories, stories I had read as a kid, and what I noticed was that his titles were all very short and direct, most of them nouns: "The Fog Horn," "The Pedestrian," "The Meadow," "The Garbage Collector," etc. That's when I remembered "The Phone Call."

"The Phone Call"—or, rather, the story that I thought "The Phone Call" could be—was perfect for the assignment. It had a touch of *Twilight Zone* in it (Bradbury wrote for *Twilight Zone*), and it also had the element of technology gone awry, a recurring theme in Bradbury's work. But could I actually write this story, twenty-one years after I had written the original version?

I could, and I did. I wrote it quickly. While the main premise remained intact, the story itself took a number of surprising turns. By the end, it was a much richer and more complex story than the one I had written in my twenties. Furthermore, it was a story that was more satisfying to write than anything I'd written in years. I had been holding this one back, afraid, I believe now, of screwing it up. (I should pause here to say that I usually end up hating most of what I write, even the stuff that's been published, because I always see the flaws in it. So, the bar for my own satisfaction is set high.) The story also retained a mother-son relationship, one in which the son is trying to save the mother, and although the circumstances are vastly different in the new version, the beating heart of the original story is still there. What had woken me in the middle of the night and led me to my typewriter remained, I'm happy to say, integral to the new version of the story I had written all those years later.

I BELIEVE THAT those pieces of writing that we never get right, the ones that make us bang our heads against a wall in an attempt to make sense of them, are the ones we haven't given enough time to gestate. Or, they are the stories that have no deeper subtext (see the chapter "Subtext"), so there's nothing deeper to plumb than what's on the surface.

If you're a student in a workshop, you may find this discouraging. How, after all, is it possible to let your stories gestate when the semester is only so many weeks long and when you have to write two or three short stories during it? For one thing, don't wait until the night before the due date to start writing your story. Begin working on your story right away. Maybe work on more than one story at a time. I do. What you want to do is give yourself the opportunity to put a completed story aside, even if for a week, in order to give it some incubation time. Then pull the story out and read over it again. You'll be surprised by how much you'll see that you didn't see right after you wrote it—odd connections, undercurrents of ideas, recurring images. What does it all mean?

And a word of advice to the budding writer eager for publication. Be patient. And listen. Your story is trying to talk to you.

EXERCISES

---

1. During the revision stage, try putting your story away for increasingly longer periods between revisions. Put it away the first time for a week. Then for a month. Then two months. Then three months. Then reverse the order of this until you're back to looking at it every day.

2. From memory, rewrite one of your stories. When you're done, read both versions. What are the differences? Did you cut anything significant from the first version? What things from the first version

had you forgotten about? Did anything minor in the first version come to the fore in the new version? Which version is better?

3. We begin constructing narratives at a young age, whether it's two Barbie dolls talking to each other or (in my case) an elaborate narrative involving Hot Wheels. Is there a story from your childhood that was ongoing? Did you ever pick up the narrative where you left off, and do you still remember fragments of that story? Try shaping one of your childhood stories into a short story for an adult audience of literary fiction.

Humility

WHEN YOU THINK ABOUT the craft of writing, you probably don't think about humility, but I would place humility at the top of that list. Humility is vital in order for a writer not to be myopic about her own work. What is humility? As defined by dictionary.com, humility is "the quality or condition of being humble; modest opinion or estimate of one's own importance, rank, etc." In regard to one's own writing, I would add that humility is an understanding that perfection hasn't yet been achieved. If the writer's life is a house, humility is the front door though which editors, professors, fellow writers, agents, and peers can enter to offer feedback and criticism. Shut that door, and you're turning your back to a world that's essential for growing as a writer: the world of advice.

Here's a story I cringe telling. When I entered college, back in the early 1980s, I was pretty cocky about my writing. Why was I so cocky? Because a few grade school and high school teachers had patted me on the head and told me how creative I was. In college, when I turned in my first poems to Rodney Jones, an award-winning poet, I expected him to tell me what a genius I was. When he began reading aloud the best student poems submitted to the class, I assumed he was saving mine for last. I waited. I watched the clock. At the end of the hour, after he had finished reading several poems that weren't mine, I assumed there had been a mistake. He must have run out of time. Or so I had convinced myself.

Rodney handed back my poems the following week, and up and down the margins he had written these three words, over and over: didactic, cliché, abstract. I knew vaguely what cliché and abstract meant but had no idea what didactic meant. My ego was instantly crushed. Who exactly *was* this guy, Rodney Jones? I went to the library and checked out his book,

The Story They Told Us of Light. I found his poems in dozens of literary magazines and read them. I saw that he had been publishing since at least the early 1970s, that he had won numerous awards, and that he had taught at a number of different schools.

My next batch of poems came back: didactic, cliché, abstract. But this time he had underlined one sentence and written, *good; concrete.* Only a couple of "good" and "concrete" words out of several poems, yet I clung to them, hoping they would unlock all the problems I'd been having, so I placed all of my poems side by side and began reading the problematic sections in groups: all of the didactic parts, all of the cliché parts, all of the abstract parts, and then, finally, the couple of good, concrete words. Instead of dashing off a poem without much thought, assuming everything I was writing was brilliant, as I had been doing, I wrote several poems, tossing one after the other away, until I wrote one that seemed unlike the others. I no longer remember what the poem was about, but I still recall the sensation of having written something that was distinctly different—my very first breakthrough as a writer, although I didn't realize that's what it had been. I didn't even know if it was any good, only that it was unlike the others.

I was nervous turning in the new poem. At the beginning of the next class, Rodney walked up to me, shook my hand, and said, "You've made quantum leaps." He handed back the poem, on which he'd written mostly positive comments in the margin. How I felt reminds me now of the ending of Anton Chekhov's short story "The Lady with the Dog":

> And it seemed as though in a little while the solution would be found, and then a new and splendid life would begin; and it was clear to both of them that they had still a long, long road before them, and that the most complicated and difficult part of it was only just beginning.

In retrospect, I realize that Rodney's praise had been generous, but it was enough to keep me going. I tell this story because if I had been committed to the view of myself as a genius, as someone who didn't need advice from someone with much more experience (an accomplished writer), I wouldn't be writing this essay today. Who knows what I'd be doing, but I can assure you I wouldn't be a writer. I tell this story, too, because it frightens me how a slight shift in attitude early on made a life-changing difference that I could not possibly have seen back then. I was too naïve, often set in my ways, so it was even odds as to whether I was going to open a door and invite Rodney Jones in or shut it in his face. I got lucky.

I've been thinking a lot about humility recently because, as a creative writing professor, I see less and less of it each year, and it depresses me. I had a student not long ago who, whenever he saw me in the hallway, would tell me about whatever story he was working on. "This one's particularly brilliant," he would say each time without a hint of irony. A few years ago, a student came up to me after the first day of a beginning short story workshop and said, "I'm afraid you're going to compromise my artistic integrity." Was he joking? I wondered. No, he wasn't. More recently, when I suggested to a student that it wasn't a good idea to begin a story in an omniscient third person point of view and then switch to first person, he bristled. "I'm a good writer," he told me. "I've read all of Hemingway." This was a student who made it a point to disagree with everything I said all semester long, raising his hand several times each class and interrupting to say, "Yeah, but . . ." I could give several dozen more examples, but I'll spare you.

In all fairness, the problem isn't just generational. I've seen it among older conference participants, aspiring writers in their sixties and seventies, who will say to me, if I mention a problem with sentimentality, "You'd understand if you had kids" or "When you've lived as long as I have, you'll know what I was talking about."

Here's something I never say in class but would like to stress here: the students of mine who've had success were, without exception, the ones who exhibited the most humility. Is this a coincidence? Absolutely not. I often tell my students that once you start getting verbally defensive over what someone's saying about your work, you permanently shut the door, unable to see grains of truth in what's been said. If you train yourself to *listen*, even if you're silently disagreeing with the criticism, you may find eventually something in those comments that proves to be the solution you've been looking for, even if it's a month or two later. When you leave the door open, there's still an opportunity to see what's valid. But when you shut it, the possibility of ever returning to those comments diminishes or disappears altogether. (I'm not suggesting that only the humble triumph, only that humility will serve both you and your craft better in the long run.)

The professionals with whom I've worked have each offered useful advice from quite different perspectives. My professors offered comments having to do with the stories' aesthetics: *Notice how the point of view slips here.* My agent's comments have often been strategic: *This would be a stronger opening chapter. Is there a way to begin it here so as to hook the editor?* My editor's comments are usually about plot and structure: *The tension is weak in the last seventy pages; is there a way to heighten it?* Maybe I'm a pushover, but I tend to agree with ninety-five percent of the comments given to me. These comments have always—*always*—made the work stronger.

But let me back up. What about humility in the composing stage? Shouldn't you feel confident and surefooted when you sit down to write? I'm not so sure. I tend to think that whatever I'm working on—whether it's a short story or a novel—is smarter than I am. It knows things I don't. How is that possible? If you're in that writing groove where words are simply appearing on the page, where characters and images are emerging that surprise even you as you're writing them, then you've probably tapped into your unconscious mind, and unless you understand how your unconscious mind works, what lurks up there, and how all the disparate images and people in your story are connected, you may want to stand humbled in its presence. This is the story or novel talking to you. The only way to figure out what it all means is to revise it, sometimes over a very long period of time, until you can catch up to speed with your unconscious mind.

I'm not trying to get all metaphysical here, but I do think that a lack of humility, at every step of the process, slams shut the door to growth. It's reassuring to see writers more famous than most of us will ever be having doubts about their own work or their talent. In the introduction to *Slow*

Learner, his collection of early short stories, Thomas Pynchon writes this of two stories in the book:

> Disagreeable as I find "Low-lands" now, it's nothing compared to my bleakness of heart when I have to look at "Entropy." The story is a fine example of a procedural error beginning writers are always being cautioned against. It is simply wrong to begin with a theme, symbol, or other abstract unifying agent, and then try to force characters and events to conform to it.

Katherine Dunn, author of the modern classic *Geek Love*, wrote this as an afterword to the book's paperback edition, and bear in mind that she's writing about a time in her life after she had already published two books with a major publishing house:

> Soon after *Truck* was published I got this lightning bolt—a Montessori moment—when I realized that I didn't know how to write. I'd been cranking the stuff all those years only semiconsciously. I opened my mouth and it poured out. It was about as deliberate and artful as belly-button lint. I was a product of that era which abhorred formal training as interference with natural expression. I'd studied history, philosophy, behavioral psychology, and biology but never had a writing class. As revelations go, this was a drag. I decided to give myself (this is the gauge of my ignorance) ten years to learn how to write.

In Kurt Vonnegut's *Palm Sunday*, a collection of essays, he actually grades his own books. He gives two A-pluses—*Cat's Cradle* and *Slaughterhouse-Five*—but he also doles out a few Ds—*Happy Birthday, Wanda June* and *Slapstick*. As for the high grades, he notes that he has compared himself against himself. "Thus can I give myself an A-plus for *Cat's Cradle*," he writes, "while knowing that there was a writer named William Shakespeare." As for the book in which this essay appears, Vonnegut gives it a C.

When I work, I keep next to me John Steinbeck's book *Working Days: The Journals of The Grapes of Wrath*. His journals weren't written to be published, so they're brutally honest. One week before finishing *The Grapes of Wrath*, Steinbeck wrote this:

> I only hope it is some good. I have very grave doubts sometimes. I don't want this to seem hurried. It must be slow and measured as the rest but I am sure of one thing—it isn't the great book I had hoped it would be. It's just a run-of-the-mill book. And the awful thing is that it is absolutely the best I can do.

If John Steinbeck felt that way about *The Grapes of Wrath*, one of the greatest American novels ever written, I think we can all, each and every one of us, afford to be more humble.

EXERCISES
- -

1. Keep a journal in which you document your daily writing struggles. Be honest about them. Write about your insecurities. Write about your triumphs. Write about both failures and successes. What you write in your journal doesn't have to be long. If you read Steinbeck's journal for *The Grapes of Wrath*, you'll notice that the entries are rather short. The important thing is to keep this document of your writing life. You may be wondering what the purpose of this is. That's hard to say. It may be therapeutic. It may help you solve problems with the project. It may end up being nothing more than the story of a certain period in your life, which may prove, many years later, to be infinitely more interesting than the story or novel you were working on at the time.

2. Tom Jenks, who taught one semester at the University of Iowa when I was a graduate student, would occasionally say about a story under discussion, "What's at stake for the author in this?" I've thought about this question a lot since then. The standard question is, "What's at stake for the *main character*?" but in most significant pieces of writing, the reader can sense that the author is also taking some personal risks. A personal risk doesn't necessarily

mean autobiographical or confessional storytelling. It may be more elusive than that. Perhaps you subconsciously avoid certain kinds of stories, a mother-daughter story, for instance, because you have had too complicated of a relationship with your own mother, or maybe you don't set stories where you grew up because you've spent your life trying to forget about that place. Write a story in which there's something at stake for you as well as something at stake for the narrator.

3. Think about a time when your ego got the better of you. Write a story that taps into that feeling. Don't be afraid to be vulnerable. Don't be afraid to make yourself look bad.

FURTHER READING

Selected Works Cited

Adams, Elizabeth E. "T. Coraghessan Boyle, The Art of Fiction No. 161." Paris Review 155 (2000).

Allison, Dorothy. *Bastard out of Carolina*. New York: Dutton, 1992.

Atwood, Margaret. "Death by Landscape." *Wilderness Tips*. New York: Doubleday, 1991.

———. "Hairball." *Wilderness Tips*. New York: Doubleday, 1991.

———. *The Handmaid's Tale*. Boston: Houghton Mifflin, 1986.

Baker, Nicholson. *The Mezzanine: A Novel*. New York: Weidenfeld and Nicolson, 1988.

———. *Room Temperature: A Novel*. New York: Grove Weidenfeld, 1990.

Barreca, Regina, ed. *The Signet Book of American Humor*. Rev. ed. New York: New American Library, 2004. ·

Barrett, Lynne. *Magpies*. Pittsburgh: Carnegie Mellon University Press, 2011.

Barth, John. "Lost in the Funhouse." *Lost in the Funhouse; Fiction for Print, Tape, Live Voice*. Garden City, NY: Doubleday, 1968.

Bausch, Richard. "Spirits." *Spirits and Other Stories*. New York: Linden Press/ Simon and Schuster, 1987.

Beatty, Paul, ed. *Hokum: An Anthology of African-American Humor*. New York: Bloomsbury, 2006.

Bell, Madison Smartt. "Customs of the Country." *Barking Man and Other Stories*. New York: Ticknor and Fields, 1990.

Blair, Walter. *Native American Humor (1800–1900)*. New York: American Book, 1937.

Boyle, Kay. *Year before Last*. New York: Greenberg, 1932.

Burroway, Janet, Elizabeth Stuckey-French, and Ned Stuckey-French. *Writing Fiction: A Guide to Narrative Craft*. Boston: Longman, 2011.

Carver, Raymond. *Cathedral: Stories*. New York: Knopf, 1983.

Chabon, Michael. "Along the Frontage Road." *The Best American Short Stories 2002*. Ed. Sue Miller and Katrina Kenison. Boston: Houghton Mifflin, 2002.

Chaon, Dan. *Await Your Reply: A Novel*. New York: Ballantine, 2009.

———. "Fraternity." *Fitting Ends*. New York: Ballantine, 2003.

Chekhov, Anton. *The Lady with the Dog and Other Stories*. Trans. Constance Garnett. New York: Ecco, 1984.

Cisneros, Sandra. "Eleven." *Woman Hollering Creek, and Other Stories*. New York: Random House, 1991.

Conrad, Joseph. *Heart of Darkness and the Secret Sharer*. New York: Bantam, 1982.

Conroy, Frank. "The Writers' Workshop." *Dogs Bark, but the Caravan Rolls On: Observations Then and Now*. Boston: Houghton Mifflin, 2002.

Cunningham, Michael. "White Angel." *The Scribner Anthology of Contemporary Short Fiction: Fifty North American Stories since 1970*. Ed. Lex Williford and Michael Martone. New York: Scribner Paperback Fiction, 1999.

Dance, Daryl Cumber, ed. *Honey, Hush! An Anthology of African American Women's Humor*. New York: W. W. Norton, 1998.

Doerr, Harriet. "Edie: A Life." *The Best American Short Stories, 1989*. Ed. Margaret Atwood and Shannon Ravenel. Boston: Houghton Mifflin, 1989.

Dunn, Katherine. "Katherine Dunn in Her Own Words." *Geek Love*. New York: Warner Books, 1989.

Dybek, Stuart. Interview. *Off the Page: Writers Talk about Beginnings, Endings, and Everything in Between*. By Carole Burns. New York: W. W. Norton, 2008.

———. "Pet Milk." *The Coast of Chicago*. New York: Knopf, 1990.

———. "We Didn't." *I Sailed with Magellan*. New York: Farrar, Straus and Giroux, 2003.

Elkin, Stanley. "A Poetics for Bullies." *Criers and Kibitzers, Kibitzers and Criers*. New York: Random House, 1966.

Exley, Frederick. *A Fan's Notes: A Fictional Memoir*. New York: Vintage, 1985.

Faulkner, William. *As I Lay Dying: The Corrected Text*. New York: Vintage, 1990.

Fitzgerald, F. Scott. *The Great Gatsby*. New York: Charles Scribner's Sons, 1953.

Flick, Sherrie. *Reconsidering Happiness: A Novel*. Lincoln: University of Nebraska, 2009.

Forster, E. M. *Aspects of the Novel*. New York: Harcourt Brace & World, 1927.

Frazier, Charles. *Cold Mountain*. New York: Atlantic Monthly Press, 1997.

Frazier, Ian. "Coyote v. Acme." *Coyote v. Acme*. New York: Farrar, Straus and Giroux, 1996.

García Márquez, Gabriel. *One Hundred Years of Solitude.* Trans. Gregory Rabassa. New York: Avon, 1971.

Gardner, John. *The Art of Fiction: Notes on Craft for Young Writers.* New York: Knopf, 1984.

———. *On Becoming a Novelist.* New York: Harper and Row, 1985.

Groff, Lauren. "Delicate Edible Birds." *Delicate Edible Birds and Other Stories.* New York: Hyperion, 2009.

Haddon, Mark. *The Curious Incident of the Dog in the Night-Time.* New York: Doubleday, 2003.

Highsmith, Patricia. "The Barbarians." *Eleven: Short Stories.* New York: Atlantic Monthly Press, 1970.

Holladay, Cary. "Merry-Go-Sorry." *Prize Stories, 1999: The O. Henry Awards.* Ed. Larry Dark. New York: Doubleday, 1999.

Irving, John. *The World According to Garp.* New York: Modern Library, 1998.

Jackson, Shirley. "The Lottery." *The Lottery and Other Stories.* New York: Noonday Press, 1991.

Johnson, Denis. "Emergency." *Jesus' Son: Stories.* New York: Farrar, Straus and Giroux, 1992.

Jones, Rodney. *The Story They Told Us of Light: Poems.* Tuscaloosa: University of Alabama Press, 1980.

Joyce, James. "Araby." *Dubliners.* New York: Modern Library, 1926.

———. "The Dead." *Dubliners.* New York: Modern Library, 1926.

———. *Ulysses.* New York: Vintage, 1990.

Kercheval, Jesse Lee. *Brazil: A Novella.* Cleveland: Cleveland State University Poetry Center, 2010.

Kerouac, Jack. *On the Road.* New York: Viking, 1997.

Keyes, Daniel. *Flowers for Algernon.* New York: Harcourt, Brace and World, 1966.

King, Owen. "Wonders." *We're All in This Together: A Novella and Stories.* New York: Bloomsbury, 2005.

King, Stephen. *On Writing: A Memoir of the Craft.* New York: Scribner, 2000.

Laken, Valerie. "Map of the City." *Separate Kingdoms: Stories.* New York: Harper Perennial, 2011.

Larson, Doran. "Morphine." *Virginia Quarterly Review* 73.4 (1997). <http://www.vqronline.org/articles/1997/autumn/larson-morphine/>.

Lethem, Jonathan. *Motherless Brooklyn.* New York: Doubleday, 1999.

McNally, John. *After the Workshop: A Novel.* Berkeley: Counterpoint, 2010.

———. *America's Report Card.* New York: Free Press, 2006.

———. *The Book of Ralph*. New York: Free Press, 2004.

———. "The New Year." *Troublemakers*. Iowa City: University of Iowa Press, 2000.

———. "The Phone Call." *Shadow Show: All-New Stories in Celebration of Ray Bradbury*. Ed. Sam Weller and Mort Castle. New York: William Morrow, 2012.

———. "Smoke." *Troublemakers*. Iowa City: University of Iowa Press, 2000.

McNeely, Tom. "Sheep." *The Atlantic* June 1999.

Minot, Susan. "Sparks." *Lust and Other Stories*. Boston: Houghton Mifflin/ S. Lawrence, 1989.

Monro, D. H. "Humor, Theories of." *Collier's Encyclopedia*. CD-ROM. Newfield Publications, 1996.

Monteiro, Luana. "A Fish in the Desert." *Little Star of Bela Lua: Stories from Brazil*. New York: Harper Perennial, 2006.

Munro, Alice. "Five Points." *Selected Stories*. New York: Knopf, 1996.

Nabokov, Vladimir. *Lolita*. New York: Vintage, 1989.

Novakovich, Josip. *Fiction Writer's Workshop*. Cincinnati: Story Press, 1995.

Oates, Joyce Carol. "Where are You Going, Where Have You Been?" *The Wheel of Love, and Other Stories*. New York: Vanguard Press, 1970.

O'Brien, Tim. "How to Tell a True War Story." *The Things They Carried*. Boston: Houghton Mifflin, 1990.

———. "On the Rainy River." *The Things They Carried*. Boston: Houghton Mifflin, 1990.

O'Connor, Flannery. *Collected Works: Wise Blood / A Good Man Is Hard to Find / The Violent Bear It Away / Everything That Rises Must Converge / Stories and Occasional Prose / Letters*. Ed. Sally Fitzgerald. New York: Literary Classics of the United States, 1988.

Olsen, Sondra Spatt. "Free Writing." *Traps*. Iowa City: University of Iowa Press, 1991.

Packer, Ann. "Horse." *Mendocino and Other Stories*. San Francisco: Chronicle Books, 1994.

Percy, Benjamin. "Refresh, Refresh." *Refresh, Refresh: Stories*. Saint Paul, MN: Graywolf Press, 2007.

Plath, Sylvia. *The Bell Jar*. New York: Harper and Row, 1971.

Poe, Edgar Allan. "The Black Cat." *Complete Stories and Poems of Edgar Allan Poe*. Garden City, NY: Doubleday, 1966.

Portis, Charles. *The Dog of the South*. New York: Knopf, 1979.

———. *Masters of Atlantis: A Novel*. Woodstock, NY: Overlook, 2000.

Pynchon, Thomas. "Introduction." *Slow Learner*. New York: Bantam, 1985.

Russo, Richard. *Mohawk*. New York: Vintage, 1986.

———. "The Whore's Child." *The Whore's Child: And Other Stories*. New York: Knopf, 2002.

Salinger, J. D. *The Catcher in the Rye*. Boston: Little, Brown, 1951.

Sebold, Alice. *The Lovely Bones: A Novel*. Boston: Little, Brown, 2002.

Simpson, Mona. *Anywhere but Here*. New York: Knopf, 1987.

Stafford, Jean. *The Collected Stories of Jean Stafford*. New York: Farrar, Straus and Giroux, 1969.

Steinbeck, John. *East of Eden*. New York: Penguin, 2002.

———. *Working Days: The Journals of the Grapes of Wrath, 1938–1941*. Ed. Robert J. DeMott. New York: Viking, 1989.

Stern, Jerome. *Making Shapely Fiction*. New York: Norton, 1991.

Stone, Peter H. "Gabriel García Márquez, The Art of Fiction No. 69." *Paris Review* 2 (1981).

Strunk, William, and E. B. White. *The Elements of Style*. New York: Macmillan, 1979.

Swick, Marly. "A Hole in the Language." *A Hole in the Language*. Iowa City: University of Iowa Press, 1990.

Teicholz, Tom. "Cynthia Ozick, The Art of Fiction No. 95." *Paris Review* 102 (1987).

Toole, F. X. *Million Dollar Baby: Stories from the Corner*. New York: HarperCollins, 2005.

Twain, Mark. *Adventures of Huckleberry Finn*. New York: Random House, 1996.

Updike, John. "The Lovely Troubled Daughters of Our Old Crowd." *Trust Me: Short Stories*. New York: Knopf, 1987.

Vonnegut, Kurt. "The Sexual Revolution." *Palm Sunday: An Autobiographical Collage*. New York: Dell, 1999.

Wilson, Leigh Allison. "Massé." *Wind*. New York: William Morrow, 1989.

Wolfe, Thomas. *The Letters of Thomas Wolfe*. Ed. Elizabeth Nowell. New York: Charles Scribner & Sons, 1956.

Wray, John. *Lowboy*. New York: Farrar Straus and Giroux, 2009.

Wright, Richard. *Black Boy (American Hunger): A Record of Childhood and Youth*. New York: HarperPerennial, 1993.

Yates, Richard. *Disturbing the Peace: A Novel*. New York: Delacorte Press/ S. Lawrence, 1975.

———. *Revolutionary Road*. New York: Vintage Contemporaries, 2000.

The Writer's Life

Bailey, Blake. *Cheever: A Life*. New York: Knopf, 2009.

———. *A Tragic Honesty: The Life and Work of Richard Yates*. New York: Picador, 2003.

Boyle, Kay, and Robert McAlmon. *Being Geniuses Together, 1920-1930*. Garden City, NY: Doubleday, 1968.

Bradbury, Ray. *Listen to the Echoes: The Ray Bradbury Interviews*. Ed. Sam Weller. Brooklyn: Melville House, 2010.

Cheever, John. *The Journals of John Cheever*. New York: Knopf, 1991.

Chekhov, Anton. *The Selected Letters of Anton Chekhov*. Ed. Lillian Hellman. Trans. Sidonie Lederer. New York: Farrar, Straus, 1955.

Cohen, Rachel. *A Chance Meeting: Intertwined Lives of American Writers and Artists, 1854–1967*. New York: Random House, 2004.

Conroy, Frank, ed. *The Eleventh Draft: Craft and the Writing Life from the Iowa Writers' Workshop*. New York: HarperCollins, 1999.

Des Pres, Terrence. "Accident and Its Scene: Reflections on the Death of John Gardner." *Writing into the World: Essays, 1973–1987*. New York: Viking, 1991.

Dillard, Annie. *Living by Fiction*. New York: Harper and Row, 1982.

———. *The Writing Life*. New York: Harper and Row, 1989.

Dubus, Andre, III. *Townie: A Memoir*. New York: W. W. Norton, 2011.

Frank, Joan. *Because You Have To: A Writing Life*. Notre Dame, IN: University of Notre Dame Press, 2012.

Himes, Chester B. *Conversations with Chester Himes*. Ed. Michel Fabre and Robert E. Skinner. Jackson: University Press of Mississippi, 1995.

Gooch, Brad. *Flannery: A Life of Flannery O'Connor*. New York: Little, Brown, 2009.

Huddle, David. *The Writing Habit: Essays*. Lebanon, NH: University Press of New England, 1994.

Kreyling, Michael. *Author and Agent: Eudora Welty and Diarmuid Russell*. New York: Farrar, Straus and Giroux, 1991.

Le Guin, Ursula K. *Dancing at the Edge of the World: Thoughts on Words, Women, Places*. New York: Grove Press, 1989.

Levine, Philip. "Mine Own John Berryman." *The Pushcart Prize, XVII, 1992–1993: Best of the Small Presses*. Ed. Bill Henderson. Wainscott, NY: Pushcart, 1992.

Lipsky, David, and David Foster Wallace. *Although of Course You End Up Becoming Yourself: A Road Trip with David Foster Wallace*. New York: Broadway, 2010.

McNally, John. *The Creative Writer's Survival Guide: Advice from an Unrepentant Novelist*. Iowa City: University of Iowa Press, 2010.

———. "Interview with Andre Dubus III." *Glimmer Train* 50 (2004).

Meade, Marion. *Bobbed Hair and Bathtub Gin: Writers Running Wild in the Twenties*. New York: Nan A. Talese/Doubleday, 2004.

Milford, Nancy. *Zelda: A Biography*. New York: Harper and Row, 1970.

Morrison, Toni. *Conversations with Toni Morrison*. Ed. Danille Kathleen Taylor-Guthrie. Jackson: University Press of Mississippi, 1994.

Nabokov, Vladimir. *Speak, Memory: An Autobiography Revisited*. New York: Putnam, 1966.

Nin, Anaïs. *The Journals of Anaïs Nin: 1931-1934*. Ed. Gunther Stuhlmann. New York: Harcout, Brace and World, 1966.

O'Connor, Flannery. *The Habit of Being: Letters*. Ed. Sally Fitzgerald. New York: Farrar, Straus and Giroux, 1979.

Pearlman, Mickey. *Listen to Their Voices: Twenty Interviews with Women Who Write*. New York: Norton, 1993.

Perkins, Maxwell E. *Editor to Author: The Letters of Maxwell E. Perkins*. Ed. John Hall Wheelock. New York: Scribner, 1979.

Sallis, James. *Chester Himes: A Life*. New York: Walker & Co., 2001.

Schiff, Stacy. *Véra: (Mrs. Vladimir Nabokov)*. London: Picador, 2000.

Solotaroff, Ted. *A Few Good Voices in My Head: Occasional Pieces on Writing, Editing, and Reading My Contemporaries*. New York: Harper and Row, 1987.

Steinbeck, John. *Steinbeck: A Life in Letters*. Ed. Elaine Steinbeck and Robert Wallsten. New York: Viking, 1975.

Tippins, Sherill. *February House*. Boston: Houghton Mifflin, 2005.

Welty, Eudora. *One Writer's Beginnings*. Cambridge, MA: Harvard University Press, 1984.

Woolf, Virginia. *The Diary of Virginia Woolf*. New York: Harcourt Brace Jovanovich, 1977.

———. *A Writer's Diary, Being Extracts from the Diary of Virginia Woolf*. New York: Harcourt Brace Jovanovich, 1973.

The Writer's Craft

Bell, Madison Smartt. *Narrative Design: Working with Imagination, Craft, and Form*. New York: W. W. Norton, 2000.

Checkoway, Julie, ed. *Creating Fiction: Instruction and Insights from Teachers of the Associated Writing Programs*. Cincinnati: Story Press, 1999.

Cheuse, Alan, and Lisa Alvarez, eds. *Writers Workshop in a Book: The Squaw*

Valley Community of Writers on the Art of Fiction. San Francisco: Chronicle Books, 2007.

DeMarco-Barrett, Barbara. *Pen on Fire: A Busy Woman's Guide to Igniting the Writer Within.* Orlando: Harcourt, 2004.

DeMarinis, Rick. *The Art and Craft of the Short Story.* Cincinnati: Story Press, 2000.

Hemley, Robin. *Turning Life into Fiction.* St. Paul, MN: Graywolf Press, 2006.

Jauss, David. *Alone with All That Could Happen: Rethinking Conventional Wisdom about the Craft of Fiction Writing.* Cincinnati: Writer's Digest, 2008.

Kercheval, Jesse Lee. *Building Fiction: How to Develop Plot and Structure.* Cincinnati: Story Press, 1997.

Leonard, Elmore. "Easy on the Adverbs, Exclamation Points and Especially Hooptedoodle—New York Times." *New York Times.* 16 July 2001. <http://www.nytimes.com/2001/07/16/arts/writers-writing-easy-adverbs-exclamation-points-especially-hooptedoodle.html>.

Masih, Tara L., ed. *Field Guide to Writing Flash Fiction: Tips from Editors, Teachers, and Writers in the Field.* Brookline, MA: Rose Metal, 2009.

O'Connor, Flannery. *Mystery and Manners: Occasional Prose.* Ed. Sally Fitzgerald and Robert Fitzgerald. New York: Farrar, Straus and Giroux, 1969.

Prose, Francine. *Reading like a Writer: A Guide for People Who Love Books and for Those Who Want to Write Them.* New York: HarperCollins, 2006.

Van Cleave, Ryan G., and Todd James Pierce. *Behind the Short Story: From First to Final Draft.* New York: Pearson Longman, 2007.

Wood, James. *How Fiction Works.* New York: Farrar, Straus and Giroux, 2008.

Woodruff, Jay, ed. *A Piece of Work: Five Writers Discuss Their Revisions.* Iowa City: University of Iowa Press, 1993.

A Few More Favorites

Alexie, Sherman. *Ten Little Indians: Stories.* New York: Grove Press, 2003.

Atwood, Margaret. *Cat's Eye.* New York: Doubleday, 1988.

Banks, Russell. *Continental Drift.* New York: Harper and Row, 1985.

Bowles, Paul. *Collected Stories and Later Writings.* New York: Library of America, 2002.

Boyle, Kay. *Fifty Stories.* New York: New Directions, 1992.

Bradbury, Ray. *The Illustrated Man.* Garden City, NY: Doubleday, 1951.

Brown, Rosellen. *Before and After.* New York: Farrar, Straus and Giroux, 1992.

Capote, Truman. *In Cold Blood: A True Account of a Multiple Murder and Its Consequences.* New York: Random House, 1966.

Carter, Angela. *Saints and Strangers*. New York: Viking, 1986.

Carver, Raymond. *Collected Stories*. New York: Library of America, 2009.

Chaon, Dan. *Among the Missing*. New York: Ballantine, 2001.

Cheever, John. *The Stories of John Cheever*. New York: Knopf, 1978.

Danticat, Edwidge. *The Dew Breaker*. New York: Knopf, 2004.

Erdrich, Louise. *Love Medicine*. New York: Harper Perennial, 1993.

Gaitskill, Mary. *Bad Behavior: Stories*. New York: Simon and Schuster, 2009.

———. *Because They Wanted To: Stories*. New York: Simon and Schuster, 1997.

García Márquez, Gabriel. *One Hundred Years of Solitude*. Trans. Gregory Rabassa. New York: Avon, 1971.

Gowdy, Barbara. *Falling Angels*. New York: Soho Press, 1990.

Haruf, Kent. "Private Debts/Public Holdings" *The Best American Short Stories, 1987*. Ed. Ann Beattie and Shannon Ravenel. Boston: Houghton Mifflin, 1987.

Hassler, Jon. *Grand Opening*. New York: William Morrow, 1987.

Himes, Chester B. *If He Hollers Let Him Go: A Novel*. New York: Thunder's Mouth, 1986.

Hurston, Zora Neale. *Their Eyes Were Watching God: A Novel*. New York: Perennial Library, 1990.

Le Guin, Ursula K. *The Lathe of Heaven*. New York: Scribner, 1971.

Martin, Valerie. *The Consolation of Nature, and Other Stories*. Boston: Houghton Mifflin, 1988.

McCracken, Elizabeth. *Here's Your Hat What's Your Hurry: Stories*. New York: Turtle Bay Books, 1993.

McKnight, Reginald. *White Boys*. New York: Henry Holt, 1998.

Millhauser, Steven. *Edwin Mullhouse: The Life and Death of an American Writer, 1943–1954, by Jeffrey Cartwright : A Novel*. New York: Knopf, 1972.

Russo, Richard. *The Risk Pool*. New York: Vintage, 1994.

Thompson, Jim. *Pop. 1280*. New York: Vintage, 1990.

Welch, James. *Winter in the Blood*. New York: Harper and Row, 1974.

Wolff, Tobias. *In the Garden of the North American Martyrs*. Hopewell, NJ: Ecco, 1981.

INDEX

Abbott and Costello, 102, 103, 110

Acker, Kathy, 43–44

adjectives, 69–73

Adventures of Huckleberry Finn (Twain), 41, 78

adverbs, 69–73

After the Workshop (McNally), 11, 134–135

Agee, James, 110

Agony and the Ecstasy (Stone), 43

Alexie, Sherman, 109

Algonquin Round Table, 108

Allison, Dorothy, 22

"Along the Frontage Road" (Chabon), 19

American Movie, 110

America's Report Card (McNally), 42, 133–134

Andy Griffith Show, 113

Angels (Johnson), 41

Anna Karenina (Tolstoy), 28

Anywhere but Here (Simpson), 21, 25

"Araby" (Joyce), 27, 48

Arbuckle, Fatty, 107

Art of Fiction (Gardner), xiii, xiv, xv, 33, 94–95

As I Lay Dying (Faulkner), 10, 17

Aspects of the Novel (Forster), 54

Atlas Shrugged (Rand), 43

Atwood, Margaret, 24, 29, 78, 94, 138

audience, 8–13

Austen, Jane, 41

authorial, 32, 100; language, 77–78

Await Your Reply (Chaon), 24

backstory, 85–87

Baker, Nicholson, 87

Balzac, Honoré de, 113

"Barbarians" (Highsmith), 18

Barreca, Regina, 108

Barrett, Lynne, 27

Barth, John, 11, 18, 19

Barthelme, Frederick, 114

Bastard out of Carolina (Allison), 22

Battle for the Planet of the Apes, 99

Bausch, Richard, 26

Beatty, Paul, 108

beginnings, 31–39; opening in specific time and place, 84–85

Bell Jar (Plath), 24, 40, 121

Bell, Madison Smartt, 22

Benchley, Robert, 108

Benny, Jack, 102

Bergen, Edgar, 99, 102

Best of Johnny Carson, 108

Bible, 41

Black Boy (Wright), 10

"Black Cat" (Poe), 80–81

Blair, Walter, 107

Bogart, Humphrey, 4

Book of Ralph (McNally), 112, 115–116, 132–133

Both Ways Is the Only Way I Want It (Meloy), 42

Boyle, Kay, 25

Boyle, T. C., 6, 109

Bradbury, Ray, 41, 138

Brazil (Kercheval), 21

Bread Loaf Writers' Conference, 53

Bridge of Sighs (Russo), 40

Brontë, Charlotte, 41

Bukowski, Charles, 5

Burns, Robert, 41

Burroway, Janet, 20

Buster and Billie, 99

Carlin, George, 103, 107

Carver, Raymond, 11, 91, 97

Catcher in the Rye (Salinger), 40, 54–61, 78

Cathedral (Carver), 11

Cat's Cradle (Vonnegut), 145

Chabon, Michael, 19

Chaon, Dan, 21, 24

Chaplin, Charlie, 102, 107

characterization: development sacrificed, 23; flat characters, 54; minor characters, 53–62; one-dimensional characters, 16; and physical description, 95–96; stick figures, 18. *See also* main character; narrator

Cheap Trick, 99

Cheech and Chong, 103, 110

Chekhov, Anton, 142

Chinese Connection, 99

Cien Años de Soledad (García Márquez), 44

Cisneros, Sandra, 20

Clancy, Tom, 47

clichés, 17, 18, 78–79

Cold Mountain (Frazier), 72

"Comedy's Greatest Era" (Agee), 110

conflict, 87

Conquest of the Planet of the Apes, 99

Conrad, Joseph, 27

Conroy, Frank, 12, 31, 82

contract with reader, 31–38

Cosby, Bill, 103

"Coyote v. Acme" (Frazier), 109

Crime and Punishment (Dostoyevski), 43

crime fiction, 67

Crumley, James, 44

Cunningham, Michael, 23, 29

Curious Incident of the Dog in the Night-Time (Haddon), 41, 124–125

Cussler, Clive, 47

"Customs of the Country" (Bell), 22

Dance, Daryl Cumber, 108

"Dead" (Joyce), 94

"Death by Landscape" (Atwood), 29

default modes, 14; and adverbs, 71; and immediacy, 64; language for flashbacks, 75; subject matters, 14–27; techniques, 27–29

"Delicate Edible Birds" (Groff), 21

details: filtered through distinct consciousness, 88–90; gratuitous, 88–90; physical, 95–96; sensory, 68–69

dialogue tags, 66

Dickens, Charles, 28, 44, 113

distance: control of, 94–95; psychic, 33–36. *See also* point of view

Disturbing the Peace (Yates), 24, 119–120

Doerr, Harriet, 87

Dog of the South (Portis), 107
Don Quixote (Acker), 43
Dostoyevski, Fyodor, 113
Double Indemnity, 29
Doyle, Arthur Conan, 41
Dunn, Katherine, 145
Dybek, Stuart, 19, 76, 114

East of Eden (Steinbeck), 10
"Edie: A Life" (Doerr), 87
Eggers, Dave, 42
El Yanqui (Unger), 42
Elements of Style (Strunk and White), 71
"Eleven" (Cisneros), 20
Elkin, Stanley, 22
Ellis, Bret Easton, 101
"Emergency" (Johnson), 74
endings. *See* plot
Enter the Dragon, 99
episodic. *See* plot
Escape from the Planet of the Apes, 99
Evison, Jonathan, 2, 3
Exley, Frederick, 25
experimental fiction, 18–19
exposition, 82–84

Fan's Notes (Exley), 25
Faulkner, William, 4, 10, 17, 18, 32, 38, 41, 95, 112
Fawcett-Majors, Farrah, 99
Ferber, Edna, 108
Fiction Writer's Workshop (Nova-kovich), 113
Fielding, Henry, 41
Fields, W. C., 99
first person. *See* point of view
"Fish in the Desert" (Monteiro), 28

Fitzgerald, F. Scott, 27, 41, 43
"Five Points" (Munro), 27
flashbacks, 85–87; and easy psychological explanations, 86; past perfect tense for, 76; transitions for, 75–76
flat characters. *See* characterization
Flick, Sherrie, 21
Flowers for Algernon (Keyes), 125
"Fog Horn" (Bradbury), 138
foreshadowing, 80–81
Forster, E. M., 54
Foster, Jodie, 117
Foxworthy, Jeff, 108
Frampton, Peter, 99
Franklin, Benjamin, 108
"Fraternity" (Chaon), 21
Frazier, Charles, 72
Frazier, Ian, 109
"Free Writing" (Olsen), 123–124, 126
Frey, James, 25
Frisch, Max, 41
Frost, Robert, 53

Gaiman, Neil, 138
Gallagher (character), 100
"Garbage Collector" (Bradbury), 138
García Márquez, Gabriel, 44
Gardner, John, vii, xiii, xiv, xv, xvii, 32, 33, 38, 63, 94–95, 100
Geek Love (Dunn), 145
genre fiction, 67
gestation, 128–130, 132–140
Ghosts of Chicago (McNally), 42
Gilligan's Island, 75
Glass, Philip, 91
Going All the Way (Wakefield), 43
Gong Show, 99

"Good Man Is Hard to Find"
    (O'Connor), 21
Grapes of Wrath (Steinbeck), 146
Gravity's Rainbow (Pynchon), 40
Great Expectations (Acker), 44
Great Gatsby (Fitzgerald), 27, 41, 43
Groff, Lauren, 21
Gurganus, Allan, 12, 67

Haddon, Mark, 41, 124–125
"Hairball" (Atwood), 24
Handmaid's Tale (Atwood), 78
Happy Birthday, Wanda June
    (Vonnegut), 145
Haruf, Kent, 114
Hazel Motes (character), 49
Heart of Darkness (Conrad), 27
*Heartbreaking Work of Staggering
    Genius* (Eggers), 42
Heathcock, Alan, 2, 4, 5
Hemingway, Ernest, 32, 38, 47, 91, 95
Hesse, Hermann, 41
High Noon, 88
Highsmith, Patricia, 18
Hirsch, Ed, 53
Hitchcock, Alfred, 117
Hoffman, Abbie, 44
Hoffman, Alice, 138
Hogan's Heroes, 109, 111
*Hokum: An Anthology of African
    American Humor* (Beatty), 108
Holden Caulfield (character), 54–61
"Hole in the Language" (Swick), 17
Holladay, Cary, 28
*Honey Hush!: An Anthology of Afri-
    can American Women's Humor*
    (Dance), 108
Honeymooners, 109

"Horse" (Packer), 18
"How to Tell a True War Story"
    (O'Brien), 58
Howard, Curly, 104
Howard, Moe, 104
Huckleberry Finn (character), 49
Humbert Humbert (character), 49
humility, 141–147
humor, 102–111

I Love Lucy, 109
I'm Not Stiller (Frisch), 41
imitative fallacy, 38, 118–126
immediacy, 63–98
In a Lonely Place (movie), 4
In Dreams Begin Responsibilities
    (Schwartz), 41
"In the Zoo" (Stafford), 29
inference, 85
Irving, John, 13, 41

Jackson, Shirley, 20
James, Henry, 108
Jenks, Tom, 146
Johnson, Denis, 41, 74
Jones, Rodney, 141–143
Journey, 99
Joy Luck Club (Tan), 40
Joyce, James, 20, 27, 48, 94
Jurassic Park (Crichton), 40

Kaufman, George S., 108
Keaton, Buster, 107
Kercheval, Jesse Lee, 21
Kerouac, Jack, 20, 21
Keyes, Daniel, 125
King, Owen, 18
King, Stephen, 3, 94

KISS, 99

Kissing in Manhattan (Schickler), 43

Knievel, Evel, 99

Kuehnert, Stephanie, 114

"Lady with the Pet Dog" (Chekhov), 142

Laken, Valerie, 21

Larson, Doran, 73–74

Last Good Kiss (Crumley), 44

Laurel and Hardy, 102, 107

Led Zeppelin, 99

Leno, Jay, 108

Leonard, Elmore, 97

Lessing, Doris, 43, 100

Lethem, Jonathan, 121–122

Letters of Thomas Wolfe (Wolfe), 3

Lifeboat, 117

"Light My Fire" (song), 99

limited omniscience. *See* point of view

Lloyd, Harold, 107

Lolita (Nabokov), 49

Lombardo, Billy, 114

Los Gusanos (Sayles), 42

"Lost in the Funhouse" (Barth), 19

"Lottery" (Jackson), 20

Lovely Bones (Sebold), 48

"Lovely Troubled Daughters of Our Old Crowd" (Updike), 51, 90

Lowboy (Wray), 24, 122–123

Macbeth (Shakespeare), 41

main character: likeability, 46–51; as victim, 22. *See also* narrator

"Map of the City" (Laken), 21

Marilyn Diptych (painting), 74

Marlantes, Karl, 41

Martin, Steve, 103

Marx Brothers, 102, 109

M*A*S*H, 111

"Massé" (Wilson), 18

Masters of Atlantis (Portis), 43, 107

Matterhorn (Marlantes), 41

McCarthy, Cormac, 100

McNeeley, Tom, 26

"Meadow" (Bradbury), 138

melodrama, 25, 36

Meloy, Maile, 42

Memories of the Ford Administration (Updike), 42

Meno, Joe, 114

"Merry-Go-Sorry" (Holladay), 28

metafiction, 18–19

metaphor, 73–75

Mezzanine (Baker), 87

Michaels, Lorne, 103

Million Dollar Baby: Stories from the Corner (Toole), 18

Million Little Pieces (Frey), 25

mimetic fiction, 64

minor characters. *See* characterization

Minot, Susan, 21

"Moby Dick" (song), 99

Mohawk (Russo), 40, 114

Monro, D. H., 106

Monteiro, Luana, 28

Moore, Lorrie, 46, 100, 109

"Morphine" (Larson), 73–74

Morrison, Toni, 97

Mortimer Snerd (character), 99

Motherless Brooklyn (Lethem), 121–122

Mukherjee, Bharati, 94

Munro, Alice, 27

Nabokov, Vladimir, 49
narrative momentum, 90
narrator: details filtered through,
    88–90, 100; likeable-likeable,
    48–49; likeable-unlikeable, 49–
    50; unlikeable-unlikeable, 50–51.
    See also main character
Native American Humor (Blair), 107
neighborhoods as setting, 112–117
"New Year" (McNally), 36–38
New Yorker, 114
Newton-John, Olivia, 99
Nobody's Fool (Russo), 40
nouns, 69–73
Novakovich, Josip, 113–114

Oates, Joyce Carol, 23, 25, 26, 49
O'Brien, Tim, 58, 81
O'Connor, Flannery, 21, 41, 49, 78,
    91, 128
Of Mice and Men (Steinbeck), 41
Olsen, Sondra Spatt, 123–124, 126
omniscience. *See* point of view
On Becoming a Novelist (Gardner),
    vii, xv
On Moral Fiction (Gardner), xiv
"On the Rainy River" (O'Brien), 81
On the Road (Kerouac), 20, 21
On Writing (King), 3
one-dimensional characters. *See*
    characterization
"One Hippopotamus" (Barrett), 27
One Hundred Years of Solitude
    (García Márquez), 44, 90, 112
Onion (newspaper), 110
openings. *See* beginnings
Ozick, Cynthia, 2

Packer, Ann, 18
Palm Sunday (Vonnegut), 145
Panic Room, 117
Paris Review, 2, 6
Parker, Charlie, 91
Parker, Dorothy, 104, 108
"Pedestrian" (Bradbury), 138
Percy, Benjamin, 95–96
"Perfect Day for Bananafish"
    (Salinger), 22
"Pet Milk" (Dybek), 19, 76
"Phone Call" (McNally), 135–138
Planet of the Apes, 99, 100
Plath, Sylvia, 24, 40, 108, 121
plot: contrivance, 26; crunching time,
    88; definition, 20, 79; documenting
    the day, 79–80; endings, 22, 23–24;
    episodic, 20; frame story, 29; rela-
    tion to space and time, 87–88
Poe, Edgar Allan, 80–81
"Poetics for Bullies" (Elkin), 22
point of view: choosing, 36–38; first-
    person singular, 28, 77; in genre
    fiction, 28; limited omniscient, 37–
    38, 49; in novels, 28; omniscience,
    27–28, 77; third-person limited,
    28, 77
pop culture in fiction, 99–101
Portis, Charles, 43, 107
Pride and Prejudice (Austen), 43
process. *See* writing process
Pryor, Richard, 103
Pynchon, Thomas, 11, 40, 144–145
psychic distance, 33–38, 94–95

Raise the High Roof Beam, Carpenters
    (Salinger), 43
Rand, Ayn, 43

Re: Colonised Planet 5, Shikasta (Lessing), 43
reader. *See* audience
Reconsidering Happiness (Flick), 21
redundancies, 68
"Refresh, Refresh" (Percy), 95–96
restraint, 17
Resuscitation of a Hanged Man (Johnson), 41
Return to a Place Lit by a Glass of Milk (Simic), 41
Revenge of the Radioactive Lady (Stuckey-French), 3–4
revision, 127–130
Revolutionary Road (Yates), 70
Risk Pool (Russo), 40
Ritz Brothers, 102
romance novel, 10, 67
Room Temperature (Baker), 87
"Roundabout" (song), 99
Rowan and Martin's Laugh-In, 109
rule-breaking, 32
Russo, Richard, 12, 26–27, 40, 94, 114

Salinger, J. D., 22, 43, 54–61, 78
Sanford and Son, 109
Saturday Night Live (TV show), 103
Saturday Night Live: The Best of Chris Farley (documentary), 108
Saunders, George, 109
Sayles, John, 42
Schickler, David, 43
Schwartz, Delmore, 41
Sebold, Alice, 48
second person. *See* point of view
Seinfeld (TV show), 110, 113
Selling Out (Wakefield), 43
sentence structure. *See* syntax

sentimentality, 16–17, 36
setting, 112–117
Shakespeare, William, 41
"Sheep" (McNeely), 26
Sherlock Holmes (character), 41
Signet Book of American Humor (Barreca), 108
"Silver Blaze" (Doyle), 41
Simic, Charles, 41
simile, 73–75
Simpson, Mona, 21, 25
Slapstick (Vonnegut), 145
Slaughterhouse-Five (Vonnegut), 145
Slow Learner (Pynchon), 144–145
"Smoke" (McNally), 133
Something Wicked This Way Comes (Bradbury), 41
Sound and the Fury (Faulkner), 41
"Sparks" (Minot), 21
"Spirits" (Bausch), 26
Stafford, Jean, 29
stakes: for author, 146–147; for main character, 19, 146
Starting Over (Wakefield), 43
Steal This Book (Hoffman), 44
Steinbeck, John, 3, 10, 41, 145–146
Steppenwolf (band), 42
Steppenwolf (Hesse), 41
Stern, Jerome, 14
stories, types of: But . . . It's All True!, 25; Day in the Life, 20; Dead Grandmother, 16–17; Frame, 29; Hearsay, 27; I'm a Lunatic but Don't Know It, 24; Main Character: Killed!, 22–23; Most Awesome Party, 21; Omniscient, 27–28; Road Trip, 20–21; Serial Killer, 25–26; Shaggy Dog, 26–27; Slice of Life, 19; Stories about

Short Stories (about Short Stories), 18–19; Surprise!, 23–24; The Big Game!, 17–18; Victim, 22
story, definition of, 20
Story They Told Us of Light (Jones), 142
Strunk, William, 71
Stuckey-French, Elizabeth, 3, 20
Stuckey-French, Ned, 20
Styx, 99
subject matter, 14–30
subtext, 18, 38, 127–131, 139
subtlety, 25
summarization, 27
Sunset Boulevard, 29
suspense, 26
Swick, Marly, 17
syntax, 90–94

Tan, Amy, 30
tension, 90
Things They Carried (O'Brien), 81
third person. *See* point of view
Three Stooges, 102, 104, 108
Titanic, 29
"To a Mouse" (Burns), 41
Tolstoy, Leo, 28
Tom Jones (Fielding), 41
Tomlin, Lily, 109
tone, 32, 100
Toole, F. X., 18
Triumph the Insult Comic Dog (character), 108
tropes, 15
Troublemakers (McNally), 133
Truck (Dunn), 145
Twain, Mark, 41, 49, 78, 107

24 (TV show), 88
Twilight Zone (TV show), 138

Ulysses (Joyce), 20
Unger, Douglas, 42
Updike, John, 42, 51, 90

verbs, 69–73; given to body part, 67–68
Violent Bear It Away (O'Connor), 41
Volt (Heathcock), 2
Vonnegut, Kurt, 145

Wakefield, Dan, 43
Walking Tall, 99
War and Peace (Tolstoy), 28, 43
Warhol, Andy, 74
Wayne's World, 75
Weller, Sam, 138
Welty, Eudora, 90, 97
West of Here (Evison), 2
"What's New, Pussycat?" (song), 41
"Where Are You Going, Where Have You Been?" (Oates), 23, 25, 26, 49
"White Angel" (Cunningham), 23, 29
White, E. B., 71
"Whore's Child" (Russo), 26–27
Willett, Jincy, 43
Wilson, Leigh Allison, 18
Winner of the National Book Award (Willett), 43
Wise Blood (O'Connor), 49
Wolfe, Thomas, 3
"Wonders" (King), 18
word choice, 96–97
Working Days: The Journals of

The Grapes of Wrath (Steinbeck), 3, 145–146
World According to Garp (Irving), 13, 41
worldview, 78, 100
Wray, John, 24, 122–123
Wright, Richard, 10
"Writer's Workshop" (Conroy), 82
Writing Fiction (Burroway, Stuckey-French, Stuckey-French), 20, 79

writing process, 17; location to write, 5–6; number of pages to write per day, 3–4; substance use and abuse, 4–5; time of day to write, 1–2; writing instrument, 6

Yates, Richard, 24, 70, 119–120
Year before Last (Boyle), 25
Yes (band), 99